Books, Babies, and Libraries

SERVING INFANTS, TODDLERS, THEIR PARENTS & CAREGIVERS

by
ELLIN GREENE

American Library Association
Chicago and London 1991

Cover and text design by Interface, Inc. Composition by Interface in Paladium and Helvetica on the MCS 9600 typesetting system.

Printed on 50-pound Glatfelter, a pH-neutral stock, and bound in 10-point C1S cover stock by Edwards Brothers.

The paper used in this publication meets the minimum requirements of American National Standard for Information Sciences—Permanence of Paper for Printed Library Materials, ANSI Z39.48-1984. ∞

Library of Congress Cataloging-in-Publication Data
Greene, Ellin
       Books, babies, and libraries: serving infants, toddlers, their parents and caregivers / by Ellin Greene.
            p.   cm.
       Includes index.
       ISBN 0-8389-0572-2
       1. Public libraries—Services to preschool children. 2. Preschool children—Books and reading. 3. Reading—Parent participation. 4. Libraries, Children's. I. Title.
Z718.1.G68   1991   91–17050
027.62 ' 5—dc20

Printed in the United States of America.

95 94 93 92 91   5 4 3 2 1

Dedicated to my colleagues
Barbara Rollock and Bernice Cullinan
and to the librarians and staff who participated in
the New York Public Library Early Childhood Project.

In appreciation,
Ellin Greene

CONTENTS

FOREWORD

Ellin Greene has converted a lifelong interest in early child development into a book certain to make a significant contribution to the work with the early childhood group in the library setting.

As project director and consultant to the New York Public Library's Early Childhood Project, funded by the Carnegie Corporation of New York, she designed a graduate course (in conjunction with faculty members of New York University) to better prepare librarians to work effectively with infants and toddlers and their parents or caregivers. Her primary observations in this text come from the course.

The historical basis for work with young children in public libraries is clearly outlined in Greene's introduction, starting with the Mothers' Room programs before World War II. Her discussion traces the development of pre-school services after Project Head Start in 1965 as well as the national interest in this age group, which sparked local public library practices and programs, such as those in the Orlando Public Library, and the development of early childhood centers in Erie, Pennsylvania; the Gail Borden Public Library Children's Center in Elgin, Illinois; the Early Childhood Resource and Information Center in the New York Public Library; and the Parent/Child Workshop and Cultural Center in the Middle Country (Centereach, N.Y.) Public Library.

Greene stresses the basis for emergent literacy in "an early environment that offers literary experience...and in caring adults who will introduce the child to literary pleasure." She concludes that the public library is a fitting resource for early childhood service to parents and caregivers and that librarians trained in theories of early learning are more effective in serving the interests and needs of the youngest library users.

There are comprehensive and up-to-date bibliographies, a discography, listings of films and videos, computer programs, and suitable toys, along with charts, program ideas, and discussion of current thought about child development by leading contemporary child psychologists.

Children's librarians and public library administrators, early childhood teachers, day-care staff, and others who work with young children and their parents and caregivers will find here practical guidelines and encouragement.

BARBARA ROLLOCK

PREFACE

This book grew out of a lifelong interest in early child development and the pleasure of working with young children and their parents and caregivers as a children's librarian in a public library setting for many years. It was in the early eighties that I developed and taught a course in library materials and services for early childhood at the University of Chicago Graduate Library School and discussed the idea of writing a teaching text with Herbert Bloom, senior editor at the American Library Association Publishing Services. Although Mr. Bloom was encouraging, it was not until I served as director of the New York Public Library's Early Childhood Project from 1987 to 1989, when the need for such a text became imperative, that I was willing to commit to the undertaking.

In 1978 the New York Public Library (NYPL) used special funds to create the Early Childhood Resource and Information Center (ECRIC) as a one-year demonstration project in library services for young children and their parents and caregivers. The services included a series of lectures by early childhood specialists, which brought to the center new parents and their babies; students from nearby New York University and its former neighbor Bank Street College of Education; teachers; authors, illustrators, and publishers of children's books; and visitors from across the country and abroad. Mothers and fathers played with their toddlers in the Family Room and got to know firsthand their children's personal responses to the many picture books and toys available. By the end of the demonstration year, ECRIC had become a vital part of the community, with a commitment from NYPL to continue the service. The center now serves as a resource for the entire library system as well as for librarians, teachers, and early childhood specialists, nationwide and internationally. More than 20,000 professionals visit ECRIC each year.

The next step was to expand services for children from birth to age three and their parents and caregivers in the branch library system. (Service to preschoolers, ages three to five, was already well established in the branch libraries.) In 1986, with input from Barbara Rollock, then coordinator of children's services; Hannah Nuba, director of ECRIC; Bernice MacDonald, deputy director of the branch libraries; and other librarians in the system, NYPL's Office of Development and Public Affairs submitted a proposal to the Carnegie Corporation of New York. Carnegie funded the proposal over a three-year period (1987 to 1989). As a former NYPL staff member and a library educator with a recognized interest in library service to young children, I was asked to serve as consultant to the project. With Barbara Rollock's retirement in 1987, my responsibilities were expanded and I became project director.

From the project's inception, the library administration and the advisory committee agreed that the project's emphasis should be on helping practicing librarians acquire a knowledge base from which they could interact more effectively with infants and toddlers and their parents and caregivers. (In October 1987 a survey of ALA-accredited graduate library education programs in the United States, conducted by Bernice E. Cullinan and me, revealed that only one school of the forty-two schools responding offered a joint degree program in library science and early childhood education. Moreover, only one school offered a course in early childhood resources and services on a regular basis. The results of the survey and informal contact with practicing children's librarians confirmed that children's librarians were not being prepared in academia to serve their clientele.)

As project director, I was asked to design and coordinate an innovative course for two groups of NYPL librarians, representing the three boroughs served by the library. The three-credit graduate-level course was developed with input from the advisory committee and New York University professors of early childhood and elementary education Bernice E. Cullinan, Angela Jaggar, and Carol Millsom. Funds from the Carnegie grant made it possible to invite guest lecturers, such as Burton L. White, director of the Center for Parent Education, Phyllis J. Fogelman, editor-in-chief of Dial Books for Young Readers, and Betty Farber, editor and publisher of *Parent and preschooler Newsletter*, to meet with the students.

NYPL's Early Childhood Project culminated in a national invitational conference, co-sponsored by NYPL and New York University (NYU). The conference, held on April 13 and 14, 1989, in New York, brought together 225 librarians, early childhood specialists, and university faculty from twenty-seven states and Canada. Judith Green of Ohio State University and her team of evaluators declared the conference "successful in raising awareness of the participants, in identifying areas of concern and direction, in supporting those who work with young children in library settings, and in laying the foundation for a network among professionals working with very young children and their caregivers." This formal assessment was reiterated in the enthusiastic responses of the attendees.

This book covers the topics addressed in the NYPL/NYU course. Chapter 1 presents a brief overview of the development of library service to young children and their parents and caregivers and the current role that libraries can play in early childhood learning and parent education. In Chapters 2 and 3, I have attempted to extract from the literature of early child development and emergent literacy basic information that will give librarians and other adults who work with young children a confidence based on reliable research as well as on intuition and practical experience. The remaining chapters are concerned with collection building, program planning, networking, and administering library service to early childhood.

My article "Early Childhood Centers: Three Models," originally published in *School Library Journal*, is reprinted in Appendix A. NYPL/NYU course goals and objectives, a syllabus, and a professional reading list can be found in Appendix B. The reading list and the footnote sources include the professional books, excerpts from books, and articles that the NYPL librarians taking the course found most helpful, plus more recent titles that I have found instructive. Within Chapter 4 are two bibliographies. The first (pages 35–48) lists 200 books that infants and toddlers seem to especially enjoy, based on comments from parents and librarians, and 100 audiovisual items—recordings, films, videos, and computer software—highly recommended by librarians working with young children. The second (pages 59–66) is the basis for an initial parenting collection of 150 books, magazines, films, and videos. In selecting these titles, I have tried to show the wide variety in subject matter and style of presentation currently available.

The conference program can be found in Appendix C, followed by Dorothy Butler's keynote speech and Jan Ormerod's slide talk, "Designing Books for Babies and Young Children," presented on April 15 during a post-conference panel discussion on the role of nursery rhymes, picture books, and films in early language development.

Throughout the book, I have incorporated suggestions, insights, and direct quotes from course participants, New York University faculty, guest lecturers for the course, and conference speakers and participants. I gratefully acknowledge the richness their contributions bring to this work.

ELLIN GREENE

ACKNOWLEDGMENTS

I am indebted to the many people—too numerous to acknowledge by name—who have made this book possible. First, I would like to acknowledge my students at the University of Chicago Graduate Library School and the New York Public Library librarians who participated in the New York University early childhood course or attended staff in-service workshops on library service to early childhood. I have learned so much from all of them, but I would especially like to thank Steve del Vecchio for gently but firmly keeping me on track with his insightful questions and comments. I would also like to thank the participants at the New York Public Library/New York University Early Childhood Conference who filled out questionnaires and generously shared their ideas, experiences, and materials. Many of the materials and photographs used throughout the text were provided by those participants.

I wish to acknowledge the conference speakers and workshop leaders, including Lawrence Balter, Bernice E. Cullinan, Angela Jaggar, and Carol Millsom of New York University; Dorothy Butler, author of *Babies Need Books*; Ann D. Carlson, Rosary College Graduate School of Library and Information Science; Christine Casey, New York State Department of Education; Kathryn Conroy, Community Service Society of New York; Mildred Dotson, New York Public Library Office of Special Services; Betty Farber, editor and publisher of *Parent and preschooler Newsletter*; Sandra Feinberg, Middle Country Public Library, Centereach, New York; Joan Brest Friedberg and Elizabeth Segel, co-directors of Beginning with Books, Carnegie Library of Pittsburgh; Maureen Gaffney, executive director of the Center for Children's Media; Steven L. Herb, coordinator of children's services, Dauphin County Library System, Harrisburg, Pennsylvania; Jan Ormerod, author and illustrator; Michael Searson, Kean College; Dorothy G. and Jerome L. Singer, Yale University; Iris Sutherland, LaGuardia Community College, City University; William Teale, University of Texas—San Antonio; Burton L. White, director of the Center for Parent Education, Newton, Massachusetts; and Sara J. Willoughby-Herb, Shippensburg University, for permission to use material from their conference presentations and published works.

I am grateful to my colleagues at the New York Public Library who served on the Early Childhood Project advisory committee: Christine Behrmann, Mary K. Conwell, Julie Cummins, Marilyn Iarusso, Bernice Mac-Donald, Hannah Nuba, Barbara Rollock, Donald Walker, and Sue Zeigler. They critiqued early drafts, contributed to the bibliographies, and made many helpful suggestions. Specific thanks are owed Susan Pine and Katherine Todd for the sections on computer programs and workshops, and Yolanda Bonitch, Mildred Dodson, and Harriet Gottfried for their contributions to the sections on outreach.

Thanks, too, to Jill Bradish and Denise Donavin for sharing the experience of the Gail Borden Public Library's Children's Center from the perspectives of librarian and parent, respectively.

Last, special thanks to Herbert Bloom, senior editor, ALA Books, for his warm reception to my proposal for this book, and to my editors, Bettina MacAyeal and Helen Cline, for nurturing it through birth with patience and faith in its promise.

The most important thing, I believe, about books for babies and very young children is that they are shared between the child and a caring adult.

Jan Ormerod

Ella Jenkins in concert at the New York Public Library Early Childhood Resource and Information Center. Photo credit: David Grossman.

1

INTRODUCTION

Historically, library service to children focused on the older child because librarians assumed that their primary audience was children *who already knew how to read*. Story hours, beginning in the 1890s, for instance, were designed for children eight years and older and were considered a form of reading guidance. Their purpose was to introduce new readers to literary pleasure in the hope that the listeners would turn to the books from which the stories were chosen and read the stories for themselves. Picture book hours for younger children were soon added, but it was not until the 1930s that picture book programs for three- to five-year-olds became a regular part of library service to children. It is also in the 1930s that we find the roots of the current focus on service to babies and toddlers and their parents and caregivers.

In 1935 Clarence Sumner, director of the Youngstown (Ohio) Public Library and author of *The Birthright of Babyhood*, started the Mothers' Room program. Sumner was a visionary who saw the Mothers' Room as "the 'builder' and 'feeder' for the Children's Room, *being the logical first unit in the program of the public library*" (italics added). The Mothers' Room was designed to encourage literature-sharing activities between mothers and preschoolers, not with the purpose of teaching young children to read, but "to impress upon their minds the pleasures of literature."[1] The Mothers' Room collection included picture storybooks and books and magazines on childcare. Later, the Youngstown library employed a lecturer on a regular basis—"two lectures every other week"—to talk to the mothers about children's reading, childcare, and family relations.

Although several public libraries established special rooms or alcoves for parents during the 1930s, the expectation that the Mothers' Room would become a national movement was not realized, for reasons that are still unclear. America's entrance into and participation in World War II was certainly a factor. When the United States entered the war in 1941, many

1. Clarence W. Sumner, *The Birthright of Babyhood* (New York: Thomas Nelson and Sons, 1936), 41–42.

mothers left the hearth to work in war industries; others worked long hours as volunteers in civil defense, hospitals, and so on. The postwar economy and national sentiment encouraged women to give up their jobs to returning servicemen and resume their homemaker role. Meanwhile, the concept of the Mothers' Room seems to have been forgotten, for little can be found in the library literature about Mothers' Rooms after 1942. Instead, attention turned to preschoolers, ages three to five. Library preschool story hours were looked on as the child's introduction to literature and art in a group setting on the child's own. Parents and other caregivers were discouraged from attending these programs, although exceptions were made. At the New York Public Library's Aguilar branch, for instance, Spanish-speaking parents, newly arrived from Puerto Rico, were allowed to sit at the back of the story hour room to observe the program. The purpose was to introduce the immigrants to English-language experiences that they could share with their children at home.

It was not until the federal government initiated Head Start programs in 1965 that attention once more turned to the importance of parents and caregivers in children's early development. Project Head Start, the government's response to pressure from the civil rights movement for programs that would give preschoolers from low-income black families a "head start" and improve their chances for success in the educational system, had uneven results. Where parents were involved, the programs were more successful. It soon became apparent that starting with three- and four-year-olds was already too late. The Harvard Preschool Project, for example, directed by Burton L. White from 1965 to 1978, clearly demonstrated the importance of a child's first three years in intellectual, emotional, and social development. White's findings substantiated the research and writings on early learning by Swiss psychologist Jean Piaget, whose work had become more widely known in the United States after World War II through translations and interpretations. This new information convinced librarians of the need to shift their orientation away from librarian–child-centered programs toward parent–child-centered programs.

In 1972 the Children's Services Division of the American Library Association (now the Association for Library Service to Children) established a Pre-school Services and Parent Education Committee. Two years later, on July 8, 1974, this committee and the American Association of School Librarians jointly sponsored the all-day program "Start Early for an Early Start: You and the Young Child" during the American Library Association's annual conference. Librarians were inspired by the innovative ideas disseminated at the program and adapted the ideas for their own communities. In 1979 the Orlando (Florida) Public Library initiated its "Catch 'em in the Cradle" program. The bibliography "B Is for Baby" and a pamphlet describing the library's services were distributed to new parents in hospital maternity wards. The library offered workshops for parents on ways of sharing literature with children and produced the popular film *What's So Great about Books?*, which is still used throughout the country in parent education programs. Some libraries went further and developed early childhood centers.

Early Childhood Centers

In the article "Early Childhood Centers: Three Models" (reprinted in Appendix A), I described the following centers, which opened between 1972 and 1978.

The Media Library for Preschoolers

The Media Library for Preschoolers (MLP) was the outcome of a study of the public library needs of preschoolers in Erie, Pennsylvania, made by Kenneth G. Sivulich, then director of the Erie Metropolitan Library, and Dale W. Craig, then extension librarian. The MLP was designed "to introduce preschoolers to the library, to channel their curiosity with stimulating media experience, and to provide an alternative to structured preschool programs."[2]

The center was funded by a two-year grant from the Library Services and Construction Act (LSCA). Because there was no suitable space in the main library, the MLP was located in a converted bank building, six blocks south of the main library. The former bank vault, newly decorated with paintings of Dr. Seuss and Sesame Street characters, became the story hour room. The rest of the large open space was divided, not by walls, but by activity areas. These included a "Listening Cave" with a built-in speaker for music, stories, and so forth; a "whatever-you-want-to-be" platform; an animal corner with live hamsters, gerbils, mice, rabbits, turtles, and other creatures; and a parents' lounge. Books, recordings, filmstrips, puzzles, toys, and games were easily accessible throughout the MLP. Lectures and films on early childhood were regularly scheduled for the parents, and parent-child programs, craft activities, "dial-a-story," film programs, and twice-a-day storytimes for the children. The MLP emphasized informal adult-child interaction stimulated by the media environment.

The innovative MLP was enthusiastically endorsed by the community, but lack of funds to continue the project at the end of the grant period necessitated relocation to the main library building and a scaling down of activities. The relocation, loss of original staff, and merging of city and county libraries (with a subsequent loss of financial support from the local school district) severely hampered the program and brought an end to the center as it was originally conceived. MLP was in operation from 1972 to 1974.

The Children's Center

The Gail Borden Public Library in Elgin, Illinois, opened its Children's Center on January 13, 1978. A grant from the Local Public Works Act of 1976 provided for remodeling the library's original meeting room (40 by 52 feet) and adding a skylighted atrium (24 by 18 feet) to create the Children's

---

2. Dale Craig, "Preschool Library Service," *American Libraries* 4:4 (March 1973): 136.

Center. Matching funds from an LSCA grant made possible both an extensive expansion of the collection and additional staff. When grant funds expired, the service was supported by the regular library budget. The center's first director, Mary Greenawalt, described the Children's Center as "an environment where parents and teachers can work with preschool children to create and support opportunities for intellectual and social growth....it is designed for adults and children communicating and interacting with each other."[3]

The Children's Center is located on the library's main floor, diagonally across from the Youth Room, which serves children six years and older. It is an inviting area dominated by a combination playhouse, climber, and slide, a favorite spot for the preschoolers, but a controversial item among visiting librarians who do not think a library is the appropriate place for young children to engage in activities designed for large muscle movement. Like the Media Library for Preschoolers, the Children's Center is divided into activity areas for browsing among its 14,000 books and more than 2,000 nonbook items. (A piano has been removed to make space for additional book shelving.) Stuffed animals based on storybook characters—Pooh, Curious George, Corduroy, the Cat in the Hat, and other favorites—sit atop the low shelving, within easy reach.

A larger parenting collection that no longer needs to be supplemented by the Adult Services Department is located in the Parents' Corner. The collection includes books, magazines, and pamphlets on parenting and childcare, a resource file on community health and recreational services for children, an annually updated booklet with information about area nursery schools and day-care centers, and an "Idea Box" (which replaces the cards) with hand-out sheets featuring simple activities, learning games, and crafts. The Children's Center sponsors workshops and seminars in parent education, but the director and staff believe their expertise lies in the selection and use of children's media.

The Children's Center serves a significant cross section of the urban community—racially, culturally, and economically. Now in its thirteenth year, the center has secured its place as an integral part of the library and its services. The library board, administration, and staff are committed to the concept of a center for preschoolers and supportive of the wide variety of activities that encourage emergent literacy.

The Early Childhood Resource and Information Center

The Early Childhood Resource and Information Center (ECRIC) of the New York Public Library is located on the second floor of the Hudson Park Branch Library in west Greenwich Village. Its neighbors include New York University, the New School for Social Research, and the Little Red School House. The center opened October 26, 1978, with funding from a bequest by

---

3. Personal interview, spring 1983.

the poet and children's book author Mary Agnes Miller. The idea for a library center that would serve early childhood needs was conceived by Barbara Rollock, then coordinator of children's services at the New York Public Library. The center was funded as a one-year demonstration project, but by the end of the year, community support was so strong it would have been inconceivable to close it. Unlike the two previously described centers, which were designed for parent-child interaction, ECRIC is oriented toward serving adults—"parents (single, teenage, grand, foster, prospective) as well as those who work in the fields of early childhood education, day care, Head Start, family day care, pre-kindergarten, and who are health professionals, babysitters, family-life educators, librarians, childcare workers, teachers, and social workers."[4] ECRIC offers three major services: (1) a resource collection of more than 12,500 books, pamphlets, periodicals, recordings, films, filmstrips, and videotapes on early childhood and a browsing collection of more than 1,000 picture books for young children; (2) an ongoing program of workshops and seminars on early childhood topics, conducted by educators and practitioners who contribute their time and expertise to the center; and (3) the Family Room, an area arranged to encourage interaction between child and parent or caregiver. The Family Room includes a picture book nook, a dramatic play area, a climber-slide, infant and toddler toys, playpens, infant walkers, rocking horses, rocking chairs, and music, art, science, and math corners.

Two outstanding reference books, *Resources for Early Childhood: An Annotated Bibliography and Guide for Educators, Librarians, Health Care Professionals, and Parents* and *Infancy: A Guide to the Research and Resources*, have been edited by ECRIC's director, Hannah Nuba, with contributions by members of the advisory committee.[5]

For a more detailed discussion of these three centers, refer to "Early Childhood Centers: Three Models" in Appendix A.

Parent/Child Workshop and Cultural Center

Middle Country (New York) Public Library's program is not a center, strictly speaking. However, the Parent/Child Workshop and the Cultural Center operate in many ways like the three centers described above. The Cultural Center, located in the branch library, is a room designed for parent-child interaction. It serves the 400 to 450 families who are graduates of the Parent/Child Workshop program.

Sandra Feinberg, head of children's services at the library, developed the Parent/Child Workshop while looking for an alternative to library toddler

---

4. ECRIC in-house promotion flyer.
5. Hannah Nuba Scheffler, *Resources for Early Childhood: An Annotated Bibliography and Guide for Educators, Librarians, Health Care Professionals, and Parents* (New York: Garland, 1983); Hannah Nuba Scheffler et al., *Infancy: A Guide to the Research and Resources* (New York: Garland, 1986).

hours.[6] Feinberg does not think toddlers are ready to sit and listen in a group and prefers a one-on-one relationship. As a young mother, she experienced the loneliness of having her first baby far away from extended family. "Young mothers are desperate for company and information," she says with feeling, more than a decade later. The Parent/Child Workshop answers both needs.

The stated goals and objectives of the program are to

increase parents' awareness of library services and materials

familiarize parents with community agencies and resources available for advice and support and thus decrease their sense of isolation

increase parents' knowledge of child development

encourage social and verbal interaction between parent and child and between children

increase circulation of library materials for use with infants and toddlers

provide a comfortable community place for parents and their young children

provide a rationale for broadening the scope of children's services to encompass parent education.

The library conducts a workshop one day a week for five weeks. The sessions run one hour and fifteen minutes and focus on a particular topic, such as language development, play, or nutrition. At each session, a resource person, such as a psychologist, physical fitness person, or nutritionist, is available to meet with parents in small groups or one-on-one. These resource people come out of the community and either donate their services or charge a nominal fee in return for the opportunity to reach the community through the library's program. The librarian functions as a coordinator—circulates among the families and encourages them to use the library's services and programs, introduces the resource person, and concludes the workshop with a circle of finger plays and songs. One of the sessions focuses on "family reading aloud" with a staff librarian serving as the resource person.

An outgrowth of the Parent/Child Workshop program is the Suffolk Coalition for Parents and Children, a group of librarians, educators, and representatives of social agencies in the county, who meet every month to focus on a particular issue, such as adoption, teen pregnancy, and infant programs. Members learn about resources, share information, and stretch their budgets by co-sponsoring rather than duplicating programs.

The above four centers, with their divergent approaches, can serve as models for librarians planning to start or to expand services to the very young.

6. Sandra Feinberg, "The Parent/Child Workshop: A Unique Program," *School Library Journal* 31:8 (April 1985): 38–41.

The Library's Current Role in Early Childhood Learning and Parent Education

In its report *Realities: Educational Reform in a Learning Society*, the American Library Association's Task Force on Excellence in Education identified two ways libraries contribute to preschool learning—"through the services, programs, and materials that help parents increase their skills and capabilities, and through programs that serve children directly."[7]

Libraries are centers for learning, and babies—current research demonstrates—have a built-in bent toward learning, a natural curiosity that is the basis of all learning. Burton White notes in his book *Educating the Infant and Toddler* that until the age of eight months or so "there is remarkable consistency of behavior among infants with regard to curiosity....from eight months on, however, divergence of curiosity behavior becomes consistently broader." Sadly, White reports seeing "two- and three-year-olds whose interest in learning seems to be severely depressed."[8] These differences seem to be related to the amount and type of interaction that takes place between the child and environment and between the child and primary caregiver.

A study conducted in 1980 by Ronald Powell, Margaret Taylor, and David McMillen of the University of Michigan clearly indicated the important role parents can play in influencing their children's reading and use of the library.[9] According to the study's findings, "statistically significant childhood variables were: amount of reading as a child, escort to library, whether the respondent was a frequent library user as a child, when library use began, frequency of mother's reading, frequency of father's reading, and library availability as a child."

Two conditions found essential for creating a reader are (1) an early environment that offers literary experience, that is, a print-filled environment (books, magazines, newspapers, etc.), and adults reading these materials, and (2) a caring adult to introduce the child to literary pleasure. The public library meets both requirements. Hannah Nuba, in her article "Turning Babies On to Books," writes: "Children who are exposed to repeated, age-appropriate experiences with books and stories learn to value literature as an intrinsic part of their lives. Librarians with their special resources and opportunity have a chance to be part of this vital process....In our service to early childhood we are sowing the seeds of literacy....we are initiating the love of literature."[10]

The librarian's expertise in selecting and using materials is unique. The librarian is not an early childhood educator, but—by training and

7. ALA Task Force on Excellence in Education, *Realities: Educational Reform in a Learning Society* (Chicago: American Library Association, 1984), 3.

8. Burton L. White, *Educating the Infant and Toddler* (Lexington, Mass.: Lexington Books, 1988), 48.

9. Ronald R. Powell, Margaret T. Taylor, and David L. McMillen, "Childhood Socialization: Its Effect on Adult Library Use and Adult Reading," *The Library Quarterly* 54: 3 (July 1984) 245–64.

10. Hannah Nuba, "Turning Babies On to Books" (New York Public Library, in-house document).

experience—the librarian is equipped to nurture the young child's curiosity through his interest in stories and books. Moreover, the goals of the profession give librarians a vested interest in the child's development of language and reading skills. The librarian is interested in the preliterate development of the child so that in time there will be a reading child, and in still more time, a literate adult. The outcome of effective service to early childhood is increased public awareness of the library as a resource for parents and caregivers, increased use of the library's services, and greater user satisfaction.

Effective service to early childhood requires librarians to be familiar with the behavior characteristics of very young children, theories of early learning, and the implications of both for service. Library service to early childhood crosses age specialty lines. The children's librarian must be as willing to work with the parent or caregiver as with the child. For optimal service, all specialties—children's, young adult, adult, and reference—must come together in the interest of the youngest library users.

On her retirement after forty years of successful work with children in a public library setting, Mary Greenawalt, then head of the Children's Center at the Gail Borden Public Library in Elgin, Illinois, said:

> The whole environment of the public library should suggest that reading is a joy. In every public library children's department, big or small, there should be a certain intangible atmosphere—an atmosphere of friendliness, a certain leisureness, and just enough courteous formality so that a young reader may feel himself an independent individual, "on his own," free for the moment from his family's or his school's expectations and pressures, loving and helpful as they may be. Added to this must be a children's librarian who smiles a greeting to each child as he enters, who never looks too busy to be interrupted, and never insists on helping someone who doesn't need help.

During the New York Public Library/New York University (NYPL/NYU) Early Childhood Conference, Steven Herb, coordinator of children's services at the Dauphin County Library System in Harrisburg, Pennsylvania, agreed with Greenawalt, stating his philosophy of library service to children as follows:

1. Children's librarians must be advocates for children.
2. Literacy has to be the root of everything children's librarians do.
3. The library has to have a profound effect on the child during the *first* visit so the child will want to come back. The child must associate the library with *joy*.

In his inaugural address, delivered June 27, 1990, ALA president Richard M. Dougherty affirmed, "We [librarians] know, better than anybody, the joy that can be attached to the search for ideas, the personal satisfactions that derive from finding desired information, the academic achievement and the business success that depends on access to information." Dougherty spoke of the role librarians can play in building a literate America and called on them to become "leading, vocal advocates for children." "Kids who read—succeed! Let that be our rallying cry for the '90s," Dougherty proclaimed.[11]

The Association for Library Service to Children (ALSC) actively supports services for very young children and their parents and caregivers through the work of its Preschool Services and Parent Education Committee. This committee prepared the leaflet *How to Raise a Reader: Sharing Books with Infants and Toddlers.*[12] ALSC sponsored a preconference, "Ring Around Reading: Infants and the Literacy Experience," before the 1987 ALA annual conference held in San Francisco, as well as "Preschool Services in the Year 2000," a panel of experts discussing the impact of changing demographics, publishing trends, and other factors on library service to young children, during the 1990 ALA annual conference held in Chicago.[13]

JOYS, the acronym for *Journal of Youth Services in Libraries*, published jointly by the Association for Library Service to Children and Young Adult Services Division of ALA, is a pleasant reminder that joy in learning and joy in nurturing our humanness are what library service to children is all about.

11. *American Libraries*, February 1991, pp. 176 and 178.

12. Floyd C. Dickson and Janice D. Smuda, Preschool Services and Parent Education Committee, Association for Library Service to Children, *How to Raise a Reader: Sharing Books with Infants and Toddlers* (Chicago: American Library Association, 1990).

13. Audiotapes of the 1987 preconference are available from acts, 1025 East Clayton Road, Ballwin, MO 63011, (314) 394-0611. Request tapes LA 8701a to LA 8701c.

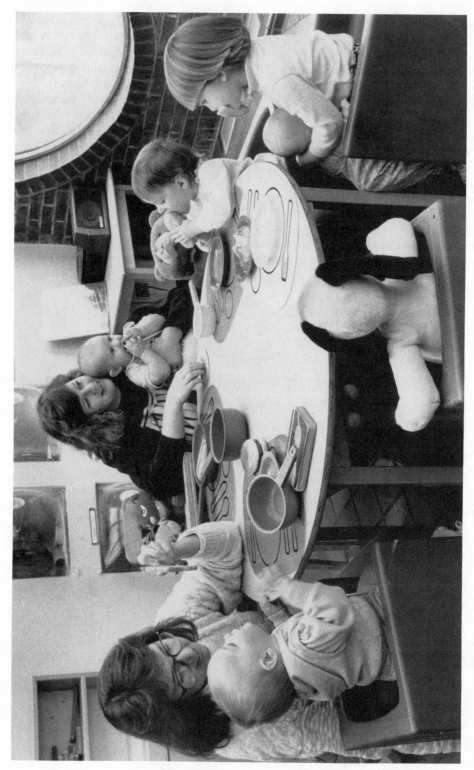

Babies and moms play in the "kitchen area" in front of the bubble window at the Children's Center, Gail Borden Public Library, Elgin, Illinois. Photo credit: Cliff E. Lohs.

2

EARLY CHILD DEVELOPMENT AND LEARNING

The twentieth century has been called the century of the child. Unfortunately, millions of children throughout the world still suffer from hunger, maltreatment, or neglect, as was noted at the World Summit for Children held at the United Nations in New York in September 1990. In the United States alone, twelve million children live in poverty, and five million are in danger of dying of hunger. And more than half a million children in our country die from child abuse each year. On the positive side, however, is the fact that our knowledge of how children develop and learn has increased tremendously in the twentieth century, and especially since the 1960s. Research has become more accurate through the use of modern technology, including videotapes and computers. We now have the knowledge to give all children "a fair start," but "that knowledge is not always available to those who care for children or who make decisions about programmes of care and development....the state-of-the-practice lags well behind the state-of-the-art."[1]

Major Theories

Early in this century, adults were shocked to learn from Sigmund Freud (1856–1939) that children are sexual human beings. Freud believed that the id, or sexual energy, drives human behavior. Erik Erikson (b. 1902), an analyst trained in Freudian doctrine, believes that the ego, not the id, motivates human behavior. His work with Native Americans and with World War II veterans convinced him that emotional distress is as much the result of cognitive conflict—the way a person thinks about himself—as the repressed sexual drives that Freud emphasized.[2] According to Erikson's theory, human development is a series of psychosocial crises that must be resolved successfully in order to mature. The first three ego crises, or stages, take place in early childhood (see fig. 1).

1. Robert G. Myers, *Towards a Fair Start for Children: Programming for Early Childhood Care and Development in the Developing World* (New York: Unesco, 1990), 16.
2. Erik H. Erikson, *Childhood and Society*, 2nd rev. ed. (New York: Norton, 1964).

Founder/Proponent	Model	Stages	Implications
Sigmund Freud (1856–1939) Austrian neurologist	Psychoanalytic id=libido, or sexual energy ego=mediator between right and wrong. superego=conscience The *id* drives behavior. Infants are amoral.	The child progresses through a series of psychosexual stages: oral (birth to weaning from breast or bottle) anal (toddlerhood) phallic (preschool)	The child derives pleasure through release of libido by means of: eating, sucking, mouthing release of body wastes masturbation, fondling, sexual fantasies about the parent of the opposite sex Caregiver must establish the parameters of what is right and wrong.
Erik Erikson (b. 1902) American psychoanalyst	Psychosocial The *ego* drives behavior and develops in response to social institutions, including family and school.	Individuals progress through eight stages, or ego crises, in which there are basic conflicts. Stage 1 (birth to 18 months): *Trust vs. mistrust*	If the caregiver meets the child's basic needs in consistent, loving ways, the child will develop a stronger sense of trust than of mistrust.

		Stage 2 (18 months to 3 years): *Autonomy vs. shame and doubt*	If the caregiver rewards the child's growing attempts at independence and doesn't shame the child's failures (e.g., at bowel or bladder control), the child will develop confidence in dealing with the environment.
		Stage 3 (3–5 years): *Initiative vs. guilt*	The caregiver needs to provide an environment in which children can engage in many activities. If the child is not allowed initiative, he will feel guilty about attempts at independence.
Arnold Gesell (1880–1961) American psychologist	Maturational Genetic and biological forces motivate development. This theory is rooted in the philosophy of Friedrich Froebel (1782–1852), the German educator and founder of the kindergarten	Development follows a sequence common to all human beings, but each child has a built-in biological schedule. Maturation is predictable, patterned, and orderly. The two main rules of development are (1) growth proceeds from the head	The caregiver should not interfere with the child's innate timetable. Neither lack of exercise nor extra training seems to have any *lasting* effects on individual growth rates. When the child is ready—i.e., has the maturation—he will accomplish the task (concept of "readiness").

Figure 1. Major Theories of Early Development

Founder/Proponent	Model	Stages	Implications
Gesell (continued)	movement. Froebel likened children to plants (kindergarten = a garden of children) and their parents to gardeners.	downward and from the center of the body to the periphery (the principle of cephalocaudad development) and (2) behavior does not develop in a straight-line direction, but in repeated alternation of immature and more mature behavior (the principle of reciprocal interweaving). Equilibrium (more mature) stages occur at ages 2 and 3; disequilibrium (immature behavior) occurs at ages 2½ and 3½.	The child learns to coordinate gross movements of his arms and legs, which are close to the trunk, before learning fine motor coordination of his fingers and toes, which are closer to the periphery. The toddler can do hand plays before finger plays. The caregiver should be prepared for unreasonableness. Try to redirect the toddler's attention. A firm hug to prevent the child from engaging in inappropriate activity usually works better than explanations or admonishments.
Maria Montessori (1870–1952) Italian physician and educator	Montessori system (cognitive-based) The child learns through the senses. He learns best in a "prepared environment" containing materials designed	The child teaches himself by self-selecting materials from a prepared environment. The three stages of learning include (1) absorbing, (2) repeatedly acting out the connections between the absorbed phenomena, and	The caregiver's task is to provide the child with sensory experiences that support learning. The caregiver needs to be aware of the child's sensitive periods in order to design an individualized program.

	to train the senses and facilitate learning.	(3) making the concept meaningful. There are genetically programmed *sensitive periods* in which the child is more capable of learning certain tasks.	Between ages 1 and 3, there is a sensitvity for order, when impressions and experiences are being placed in ordered patterns. Sensitivity for language occurs between ages 3 and 5½; for coordination of movement between 2½ and 4; for social relations between 2½ and 5.
B.F. Skinner (1904–90) American psychologist	Behavioral There is no genetic plan of development. Learning and growth occur in response to external stimulation and the reward system inherent in the environment (operant conditioning).	The child is unprogrammed and learns by reactions to stimuli and reinforcement. Behavior that is rewarded by the child's environment becomes dominant over behavior that is either punished or not rewarded.	The caregiver should arrange the child's environment so that it facilitates, shapes, and rewards desired behavior. The caregiver can control behavior by providing appropriate and immediate rewards for desired behavior, such as verbal praise, affection and use of toys. The caregiver should model and demonstrate desired behavior.

Figure 1.   (continued)

Founder/Proponent	Model	Stages	Implications
Jean Piaget (1896–1980) Swiss psychologist	Cognitive-developmental	Cognitive development occurs in orderly, sequential stages for all persons, but the age varies depending on the biological maturation and experience of the individual.	The caregiver's task is to provide the child with an enriched environment.
	Learning occurs through interaction with the environment. The child organizes his thoughts or motor activities in units of knowledge, or *schemes*. Through the processes of assimilation (absorbing the experience) and accommo-dation (adapting the old experience to the new), the child modifies his schemes (i.e., learns).	Sensory-motor stage (birth to 2 years)	The child learns through his senses and by manipulating objects.
		Preoperational stage (2–7 years)	The child begins to use speech to communicate. His thinking is characterized by egocentrism (the inability to take another person's point of view) and animism (the belief that inanimate objects are alive).

Figure 1. (continued)

Arnold Gesell (1880–1961), an American psychologist long associated with the Yale Clinic of Child Development, believed that maturation, or biological forces, determines the rate and time at which development and learning take place. Development is patterned, predictable, and measurable. In 1928, based on his observations of young children at the Yale Clinic, Gesell published his tests for infants and preschoolers under the title *Infancy and Human Growth*. These tests, periodically revised to reflect current findings, are used throughout the world to measure development in four areas: motor, adaptive, language, and personal-social.[3] A century earlier, Friedrich Froebel (1782–1852), the German educational reformer and founder of the kindergarten movement (1840), also propounded the theory of maturation. Growth was an "unfolding" and proceeded in an orderly, predictable sequence.

Other theorists emphasized the environment as the determining force. Maria Montessori (1870–1952), an Italian physician and educator, believed that children are born with psychic powers that enable them to teach themselves. Young children unconsciously absorb the culture around them. The task of the adult is to "prepare the environment to help the infant mind in the work of development." The "prepared environment" includes child-size furnishings and specially constructed materials used by the child in play activities designed to give the child real-life experience.[4] Pouring water through a funnel, scrubbing a table top, sweeping sawdust, grouping and counting beads, handling a book, and similar play activities provide sensory experiences for safely exploring the world. Montessori developed self-teaching materials for young children. Some of the materials are expensive, but many can be hand-made (see page 69 for catalog address).

The behaviorists, led by John B. Watson (1878–1958) in the early 1900s, attempted to establish a *science* of behavior by observing responses under controlled conditions. Watson's emphasis on stimulus-response, or the more mechanical aspects of behavior, sometimes resulted in a narrow interpretation of behaviorism. Since World War II, the name most associated with behaviorism has been Burrhus Frederic (B. F.) Skinner (1904–90). According to Skinner, learning is the result of a person's interaction with the physical and social environment *and* the reinforcement or reward system of that environment (operant conditioning).[5] His principles of operant conditioning led to programmed instruction and teaching machines. Skinner achieved notoriety of sorts in 1945 when news of his "baby-tender," or air crib, was reported in *Ladies Home Journal*.[6] Skinner invented the air crib to simplify the

3. See Louise Bates Ames et al., *The Gesell Institute's Child from One to Six: Evaluating the Behavior of the Preschool Child* (New York: Harper, 1979).

4. Maria Montessori, *The Absorbent Mind*, trans. from the Italian by Claude A. Claremont (New York: Holt, 1967). See also David Gettman, *Basic Montessori: Learning Activities for Under-Fives* (New York: St. Martin's Press, 1987).

5. B. F. Skinner, *About Behaviorism* (New York: Knopf, 1974). The reader is also referred to Skinner's three-part autobiography *Particulars of My Life* (Knopf, 1976), *The Shaping of a Behaviorist* (Knopf, 1979), and *A Matter of Consequences* (Knopf, 1983).

6. "Baby in a Box: The Machine Age Comes to the Nursery," *Ladies Home Journal* 62 (October 1945): 30–31, 135–136, 138.

care of his second child, Debbie. The baby-tender was a crib-sized living space with sound-absorbing walls and a large picture window made of safety glass. A curtain shielded Debbie from bright light when she was sleeping. Air entered through filters and was warmed and moistened so that Debbie was comfortable wearing only a diaper. The infant was free to move about; she was taken up for feedings, and at about six months, she also spent about one and a half hours a day in a playpen or teeter-chair. Debbie spent the first two and a half years of her life in the baby-tender, apparently with no ill effects.

Albert Bandura (b. 1925) and other social learning theorists adhere to many principles of behaviorism, but emphasize the role of social interaction in the process of learning.[7] They believe learning occurs through modeling, observation, vicarious experiences, and self-regulation. Children model people who are important to them.

John Bowlby (1907–90), an English psychiatrist and behaviorist, contributed to our knowledge of child development through his studies on emotional bonding, or attachment.[8] Bowlby's studies demonstrated that infants will attend to any person nearby during the first eight weeks of life. From eight weeks on, babies begin to discriminate between familiar persons (parents or caregivers) and unfamiliar persons. By six months of age, the infant has become attached to the primary caregiver. This relationship increases in intensity during toddlerhood, forming what Burton White calls the first love affair in a human's life.

T. Berry Brazelton (b. 1918), a professor of pediatrics at Harvard Medical School and chief of child development at Boston Children's Hospital, also focuses on early relationships in his popular parenting books.[9]

Without doubt, the most influential child psychologist of the twentieth century was Jean Piaget (1896–1980) of Switzerland. Piaget's observations of his own children led him to conclude that young children organize, structure, and restructure experiences in accordance with existing schemes of thought and modify these schemes in the course of interacting with the physical and social world. Piaget used the terms "assimilation" and "accommodation" to describe this process. Children learn in developmental stages, from the concrete to the schematic to the symbolic (see fig. 1). Very young children (birth to age two) are at the concrete stage and learn by handling real objects. At the schematic stage (ages two to four), children can relate a picture of an object to the real object. Traditionally, librarians have worked with children who are at the schematic or symbolic level of development. Today, librarians understand the importance of working with children at the concrete level. (Coincidentally, teachers and librarians have discovered that older children continue to learn from manipulating materials; this is especially true of children with special needs.)

7. Albert Bandura, *Social Learning Theory* (Englewood Cliffs, N.J.: Prentice-Hall, 1977).

8. John Bowlby, *Attachment and Loss*: Volume 1, *Attachment* (New York: Basic Books, 1969).

9. For example, see T. Berry Brazelton, *Infants and Mothers: Differences in Development* (New York: Delacorte, 1969) and T. Berry Brazelton and Bertrand G. Cramer, *The Earliest Relationship: Parents, Infants, and the Drama of Early Attachment* (Reading, Mass.: Addison-Wesley, 1990).

Piaget's writings are difficult reading (he summarizes his theories in *The Psychology of the Child*), but there are some excellent interpretations, written primarily for parents, such as Mary Ann Pulaski's *Your Baby's Mind and How It Grows: Piaget's Theory for Parents* and *A Piaget Primer: How a Child Thinks*, by Dorothy Singer and Tracey Revenson.[10]

The emphasis of this chapter is on cognitive and language development, but it should be noted that motor, cognitive, language, and social development are interrelated. Motor development affects the child's language development, for instance, not only in that certain muscles need to be developed in order for speech to occur, but also in more subtle ways. An active child *attracts* the parent's attention by crawling, walking, and so on. A physical handicap that restricts the child from being actively involved in his environment may in turn affect his parent's response to him.

Behavior Characteristics of Very Young Children and Their Implications for Library Service

What are infants and toddlers like? This section contains brief descriptions of their behavior and the implications for library service to early childhood. If you have never taken a course in child development, or if you took one more than ten years ago, you will want to read a good introductory text, such as *Education and Development of Infants, Toddlers, and Preschoolers*, by George Morrison, or *Educating the Infant and Toddler*, by Burton White.[11] Familiarize yourself with the titles recommended for the parenting collection on pages 59–66 as well as the titles on the professional reading list in Appendix B. Children's book titles mentioned below are listed in the bibliography following chapter 4 on collections.

Birth to Six Months

During the first six months of life, baby is concerned primarily with adapting to her new environment, developing a relationship with the primary caregiver, and gaining control over her body. Much of her time is spent sleeping. She likes soothing, gentle sounds; enjoys being held and rocked; explores the world with eyes, ears, hands, feet, and mouth; cries to express feelings of discomfort; plays with sounds—babbles, coos, gurgles, and squeals; and begins to show preference for certain people, objects, and events.

10. Jean Piaget and B. Inhelder, *The Psychology of the Child* (New York: Basic Books, 1969); Mary Ann Pulaski, *Your Baby's Mind and How It Grows: Piaget's Theory for Parents* (New York: Harper, 1978); Dorothy G. Singer and Tracey A. Revenson, *A Piaget Primer: How a Child Thinks* (New York: New American Library, 1978).

11. George S. Morrison, *Education and Development of Infants, Toddlers, and Preschoolers* (Glenview, Ill.: Scott, Foresman, 1988); Burton L. White, *Educating the Infant and Toddler* (Lexington, Mass.: Heath, 1988).

This 5-month-old baby is completely absorbed in sharing a book with Mom. Success by 6 program, Minneapolis Public Library and Information Center. Photo credit: Judy Olausen.

Librarians can help parents and caregivers by making available quality books on parenting and appropriate children's literature, such as lullaby and song books, Mother Goose rhymes, and books showing objects, patterns, and other stimuli. Librarians can also encourage parents and caregivers to talk, sing, and read to their infants. Lap reads can begin when baby can support her own head, at about three months of age. Before then, parents and caregivers can open a book and stand it about ten inches from baby's face when she is lying on her tummy on the floor. Parents should use stiff cardboard books that stand up when opened. For lap reads at home, cloth and soft vinyl books are more appropriate because to baby a book is an object to be explored through chewing or sucking.

Seven to Fourteen Months

At about seven or eight months, children begin, as White says, "to learn language." The focus shifts from interest in the sounds of words to their meaning. The older infant continues to imitate sounds and words, but now his babbling has become "expressive jargon." He understands most of what is said to him (receptive language), but his vocabulary is likely to be limited to "bye-bye," "Ma-ma," and "Da-da" (expressive language). A favorite activity is emptying cupboards and containers—objects are to bang, shake, bite, and drop! He can pull himself up to sit or stand. He likes to climb onto the caregiver's lap and be read to. He is now capable of turning stiff, thick pages of board books—cloth books have become difficult to handle. He shows more interest in the story, but is still absorbed by pointing and naming objects in books. The child can follow simple directions, such as "touch your nose." He enjoys playing turn-taking games, such as "pat-a-cake" and "peek-a-boo." He is beginning to be independent and to show emotions like jealousy and affection, especially if there is a new baby in the family. Some librarians offer parent-child programs at this stage, with the purpose of introducing parents and caregivers to appropriate literature-sharing materials and demonstrating ways of sharing such materials with infants. Such programs should run no longer than fifteen to twenty minutes and include rhymes, songs, hand games, and very short stories. Books like *Goodnight Moon*, by Margaret Wise Brown, *Clap Hands*, by Helen Oxenbury, and *Who Said Meow?*, by Maria Polushkin, are enjoyed.

Fifteen to Twenty-four Months

Most children begin to walk during this period. They like taking things apart and attempting to fit the pieces together again. Action toys that move or make sounds are popular. Young toddlers talk in simple sentences and enjoy watching and listening to people speaking. "What's that?" and "Why?" are frequently asked, but may represent an early attempt at social communication rather than a search for information. This is the period when the parent or caregiver has a strong influence over the child's development. The young toddler is capable of thinking things through. She is beginning to assert herself—her favorite word is "NO!" She enjoys tactile books and books she can manipulate. She likes to "read" the pictures in books and may engage in reading-like behavior (holding the book and telling the story to herself). Looking and listening to *live* language (that is, between persons, not on television) are crucial activities from now through the third year, when language development can make remarkable strides.

Children this age enjoy listening to music and moving to rhythm (see Fig. 2). Puppets and flannel board stories are popular. Favorite stories include *The Very Hungry Caterpillar*, by Eric Carle, *Have You Seen My Duckling?*, by Nancy Tafuri, and *Max's Ride*, by Rosemary Wells. This is the ideal time to introduce parent-child literature-sharing programs in the library (see chapter 5, Program Planning). Because toddlers associate

Age	2 to 9 months	9 months to 2 years	2 to 3 years
Musical Development	Begins to listen attentively to musical sounds; is calmed by human voices. Starts vocalizations, appearing to imitate what he hears.	Begins to respond to music with clear repetitive movements. Interested in every kind of sound; begins to discriminate among sounds and may begin to approximate pitches. Most attracted to music that is strongly rhythmic.	Creates spontaneous songs; sings parts of familiar songs; recognizes instruments and responds more enthusiastically to certain songs. Strong physical response to music.
Activities	• Rock and sing to your baby. • Introduce a variety of rhythmic sounds, such as rattles, music boxes and rhymes.	• Dance your baby up and down on your knee or in your arms while singing rhythmic chants and songs. • Give your child simple percussion instruments, such as drums, rattles, and jingle bells, for sound exploration. • Sing and chant nursery rhymes and repetitive folk songs during various daily activities.	• Let your child hear different musical instruments. • Lead your youngster in simple imitative musical games such as "Old MacDonald Had a Farm." • Teach some simple finger plays, for example, "The Eensie Weensie Spider."

Figure 2. Chart of musical development with suggested activities

Adapted from a musical development chart by Mitzie Collins for *Parent and preschooler Newsletter.* Copyright 1987. Reproduced by permission of Preschool Publications, Inc., P.O. Box 1851, Garden City, NY 11530.

persons with places and places with persons, the same librarian—schedule permitting—should present all of the storytime programs in a series.

Twenty-five to Thirty-six Months

The child's interests are expanding. The older toddler can understand simple concepts, count, and name colors. He notices changes in the natural world, such as the seasons. He is hooked on words and relishes using new ones. By the time he is three years old, he may know as many as 1,000 words and understand 75 percent of the language he will use for the rest of his life in ordinary conversation (White). White reports an increasing interest in age-mates during this period, but this happens only when there are opportunities for interaction with other children. Though children at this age are social, parallel play is still more common than cooperative play. Many have imaginary playmates.

Older toddlers like to dress up and engage in dramatic play. They like to draw and paint and are interested in textures and shapes. Favorite playthings include push and pull toys, pile-up toys, toy telephones, plastic containers with lids, puzzles with few pieces, musical toys, record players, blocks, crayons, finger and brush paints, clay, and play dough. Most of these materials are appropriate for the early childhood area in the library.

If the librarian is not already offering parent-child literature-sharing programs, now is the time to begin. Toddlers can follow a simple plot. They recognize and remember characters and scenes. Two- and three-year-olds spend a lot of time looking at the pictures in books. They enjoy concept books, such as *Freight Train*, by Donald Crews, and *Push Pull, Empty Full*, by Tana Hoban; family stories, such as *Alfie Gets in First*, by Shirley Hughes, and *The Snowy Day*, by Ezra Jack Keats; and stories that invite participation, such as that old favorite *Brown Bear, Brown Bear, What Do You See?*, by Bill Martin and John Archambault. Older toddlers like stories about messy eaters, getting lost, and going to bed. Predictable stories that have a lot of repetition and rhyme are good choices for the storytime.

Encourage parents to talk with their children about the stories they read together and to enjoy the inevitable changes in the way their children respond to the same stories over a period of time. Parents need to know that this interaction is one of the most important things they can do to encourage emergent literacy.

Enjoying books at the New York Public Library Epiphany Branch. Photo credit: David Grossman.

3

EMERGENT LITERACY

"When—and how—shall I teach my child to read?" is probably the most frequently asked question of the children's librarian by new parents.

The Parent's Role

Educators once believed that children were unable to learn to read until they reached a certain level of physical and mental development, which occurred at about six years of age. The current theory, based on studies of early readers (children who taught themselves to read before beginning school), is that human beings learn to read in much the same way they learn language; that is, they learn in context through interaction with a caring adult. The acquisition of literacy is now viewed as a social process and, consequently, the role of parent-child interaction has assumed greater importance. The process begins at birth (some contend it begins during the prenatal period, when the unborn child becomes conditioned to its mother's voice). Reading is an oral-language-based skill; it is communication; it has meaning. When an adult shares a book with a child and asks, "What do you think will happen?", the adult is articulating the process of reading—to predict, to look for more information, to respond, to wonder.

Brian Cambourne summarized the conditions under which children can learn to read and write as naturally as they learn to talk. These conditions include immersion, demonstration, expectation, responsibility, approximation, employment, and feedback.[1]

1. Brian Cambourne, "Language, Learning and Literacy," in *Towards a Reading-Writing Classroom*, ed. Andrea Butler and Jan Turbill (Portsmouth, N.H.: Heinemann, 1987).

Sections of this chapter were published in slightly different form in the article "Books, Babies, and Libraries: The Librarian's Role in Literacy Development," by Bernice E. Cullinan, Ellin Greene, and Angela Jagger, *Language Arts* 67:7 (November 1990): 750–55. Copyright 1990 by the National Council of Teachers of English. Reprinted with permission.

Immersion

Babies respond to the sounds of language even before they learn to associate sounds with meanings. During their child's first six months of life, parents can encourage interest in the sounds of language by singing and talking to baby. Although babies cannot talk, they can and do respond to human speech through sounds and body movements. At about seven or eight months of age, baby's attention shifts from interest in the sounds of words to the meanings of words. "Words are finely tuned instruments which must be encountered early if their shades of meaning are to serve the developing intellect and emotions," asserts Dorothy Butler. "Babies and small children need precision, beauty, lilt and rhythm, and the opportunity to look and to listen, both at will and at length, as well as to touch and feel and smell."[2]

As soon as baby can sit with support, the parent can hold him on her lap and read aloud from board books that have bright, clear pictures of familiar objects, animals, and people. At about fifteen months, the child will begin joining in the reading by turning the book's pages for the adult. At this stage, he enjoys pointing to the pictures and asking, "What's that?" Between the ages of two and three, he may hold a book and "read" the story out loud, often using the exact words in the book or coming to a close approximation.

Demonstration

Every time adults use language around a child, they are giving demonstrations of the functions of language—that is, how language is used and what it is used for. They demonstrate the richness of language when they use a broad vocabulary. They demonstrate intonation, the way a raised tone indicates additional meaning. And they demonstrate language structure, its grammar. They use language in a variety of ways for a variety of reasons. Language varies in form, structure, and function, and children learn these aspects of language from the demonstrations and models around them. Infants are born with the capacity to learn any language, but by the end of their first year, they are oriented to learn a particular language—that is, the dominant language of their culture.

Approximation

When we learn a new skill, our attempts to reproduce the skilled demonstrations we observe are not very much like the models. These attempts are called approximations. In language learning, children make approximations of what they hear. The first sounds of "Mmmmm" or "Dada" are approximations of the words "Mama" and "Daddy." Parents are delighted and accept their children's approximations with parental pride. Children

2. Dorothy Butler, "Saying It Louder," *School Library Journal* 35:13 (September 1989): 156. Reprinted in Appendix C.

learning to read make approximations of reading; we call these reenactments. If we accept children's early attempts to read and write with the same enthusiasm we show for their early attempts to talk, they will risk making more attempts.

When children are learning to write, they use "invented spelling."[3] That is, they spell words the way they sound. A seven-year-old wrote:

> Once there was a boy named Peter. One morning he got up out of bed and was geting drest when he saw he lost his socks. He lost his faerit paer of socks that he got for chrimis from his ante. He said it was the werst time of his life. Peter went downstares and toled his unle Fred he toled him that he lost his best paer of socks. His unle Fred went to look for them with Peter. they looked and looked and looked but they never fowned them because the cat had them but they didn't know that so they kept on looking and looking but still they never fowned them. Fonlle 100 people lived there so it had to be a big house and all the people were looking but not one sock was fowned. Fonlle a posern yelld I fowned them and Peter yelled yaaaaaa and peter never lost his socks agien because the cat alwes had them and peter lived happyll ever after. THE END writtin by Jason Russell Ream.

Employment and Use

Children, like adults, need a lot of practice to learn any skill. When children learn to talk, they are not restricted to twenty or thirty minutes a day for practice. Children practice talking all day long, even after they are put to bed. We do not force them to wait until "talking time" to practice their new-found skill. Likewise, children learning to read and write should not be restricted to limited periods of practice.

Cambourne's other conditions—expectation, responsibility, and feedback—are essential to literacy learning. When a child is born, parents *expect* her to learn to talk and walk. Expectations are subtle messages that we give learners about their probability of success. If we expect children to learn to read and write and we provide the same conditions that prevailed when they learned to talk, they will accomplish these literacy skills with the same ease. When a child learns to talk, she is responsible for what she will learn next. No one else sets out a sequence of skills or sounds or words. The child takes *responsibility* for determining her own language learning. The adult's job is to immerse the child in language, give continual demonstrations, expect the child to learn, and give her responsibility for determining what she will learn. Children are active learners; they need choice and responsibility for what they learn.

Feedback underscores the notion that learning language and language-related skills, such as reading and writing, is a social process. Children need to interact with others using books as a catalyst for spoken exchange; some

3. Jerome C. Harste et al., *Language Stories and Literacy Lessons* (Portsmouth, N.H.: Heinemann, 1984).

believe that the talk surrounding books is more important than the books themselves. There can be great joy in the interplay between adult and child during book reading. The book becomes a vehicle for communication, bringing adults and children physically and emotionally close. Reading aloud allows us to slow down in our fast-paced society and to rediscover our humanity in the world of story. In a discussion group, a single mother described how she took five minutes to read to her children as soon as she got home from work, even though she longed to take a warm bath and relax for a few moments before making dinner. She said the ritual had a calming effect on both herself and the children and made for a more relaxed evening. Another person in the group commented, "With working parents, lap reading may be the only time the parent belongs to the child."

The Librarian's Role

Librarians can help by encouraging parents to read aloud to their children from infancy until the children become fluent readers—and beyond—by introducing parents to quality children's books that are developmentally appropriate and by modeling how to read aloud to young children. Most libraries have toddler storytimes during the day; many offer bedtime story hours in the evening, when working parents are free to bring their children. These literacy events are important. Gordon Wells, who calls children "meaning makers," cites the differences among children in literacy abilities depending on the number of literacy events in their lives. Wells describes one child who had engaged in more than 5,000 literacy events between the ages of two and five; he excelled when he entered school and continued to excel over children who had engaged in no or few literacy events during their preschool years.[4]

Librarians and teachers need to recognize the impact of their modeling behavior and the truth of Bill Teale's statement, "There is no one *right* way to read a book with a child." Librarians traditionally read a story straight through in order to maintain its literary integrity. Nursery school teachers, on the other hand, often interact with children during read-aloud sessions by asking questions and encouraging comments. When a parent reads aloud, he holds the toddler or preschooler on his lap, focuses attention on the book, and interrupts the reading to talk about what is happening. The parent's interruptions occur at places in the story where the child might not have the experience required to understand. The parent fills in, asks questions, or "scaffolds" the learning. The child's questions, quizzical looks, or misstatements show the adult what the child needs to know in order to understand the story.

Library literacy programs for young children can be shaped around three aspects of practice developed in New Zealand and Australia: reading to,

4. Gordon Wells, *The Meaning Makers: Children Learning Language and Using Language to Learn* (Portsmouth, N.H.: Heinemann, 1986).

reading with, and reading by children.[5] Reading *to* children is a natural part of library programs. Children take delight in hearing stories and informational books read aloud. They learn book language, story patterns, literary conventions, and interesting concepts about their world from being read to. Reading *with* children, called shared reading or lap reading, occurs with an individual or a small group in which each child can see the print, read along at times, and participate in the reading process. Finally, reading *by* children is the independent practice so necessary to fluency. This requires an abundance of material that children can "zoom through with joyous familiarity," according to Bill Martin, Jr. Young readers need easy books with predictable language, repeated phrases, strong story patterns, and clear expository texts to support independent reading. Library collections can offer materials that present just the right amount of challenge for young children.

Approaches to Reading

Librarians should be knowledgeable about the different approaches to teaching reading and which methods are used in local schools. What is the literate environment at school? Is the curriculum literature-based? Are basal readers, trade books, or both used in teaching reading? What strategies or activities are employed to invite reader response? The controversy over phonics versus whole-word method continues, but recent research gives credence to the holistic point of view. The whole-language approach—where reading begins with stories rather than with letters and words, that is, with language and not decoding—has been adopted by many schools today. Whatever the methodology, it is important to emphasize to parents that children who grow up in homes where there are books and magazines and parents who obviously enjoy reading are more likely "to take to reading." Immersed in printed matter, the children soon emulate their parents' behavior. The single most important factor in learning to read in the conventional sense, according to the report of the Commission on Reading, is being read to in early childhood.[6]

In *Learning to Read and Write*, author Ellen Brooks comments:

> Theories of the reading process are often categorized as "top down" vs. "bottom up." The top down point of view stresses comprehension and meaning. The reader begins with a broad idea of what might be on the page of text and uses this as a guide to create meaning. Reasoning from whole to part characterizes the top down perspective.
>
> In contrast, proponents of a bottom up model assert that the reader reasons from part to whole, moving from sounds to words, to phrases,

---

5. Don Holdaway, *The Foundations of Literacy* (Portsmouth, N.H.: Heinemann, 1979).
6. R. C. Anderson et al., *Becoming a Nation of Readers: The Report of the Commission on Reading* (Champaign, Ill.: Center for the Study of Reading, 1985).

and finally meaning. This perspective places greater emphasis on decoding.

While these two perspectives appear to be in direct opposition...both models may be useful in reflecting the process, but at different developmental stages. The mature, fluent reader can bypass the step-by-step aspects of the decoding process and attend directly to meaning....But for the child who is just beginning to learn to read, the decoding skills are not yet automatic. As a result, much if not all of the child's attention is directed toward cracking the code. This helps us to understand the young child who reads a sentence slowly and deliberately, seeming to proceed word by word. Although each word is labeled correctly, by the time the child reaches the end of the sentence, he has forgotten the beginning and has no idea what the sentence is about. The reading task is much too complex at this point to focus on both decoding and meaning....Teachers can provide a balanced experience for the beginning reader by frequently reading to the child. In this way, the child can attend directly to meaning, and the reading as meaning orientation need not (and indeed should not) be delayed until the child becomes a more independent reader.[7]

The film *The Foundations of Reading and Writing* shows how the "artful scribbles" of young children are a prelude to writing. "Just as babbling precedes language the scribbles and sketches lay a foundation for the later acquisition of writing."[8] Art activities can help children to recognize shapes and to make meaning of symbols—both prerequisites for learning to read. Angela Jaggar recommends that libraries have writing stations to encourage children to practice putting their own ideas on paper. If space is not available for writing stations, librarians can post children's writings on the bulletin board, display books made by the children, and encourage parents to make books with their children.

Children need to recognize the forms of written language if they are to succeed in reading and writing. Common literary devices such as "once upon a time" and "they lived happily ever after" are not constructions that children hear in their daily lives unless they are read to by someone.

We can see into children's storehouses of language possibilities when they talk, tell stories, and write.[9] We can see reflections of the language they have heard, the literature they have read or have had read to them, and what they have taken for their own. A first-grade girl wrote the following:

7. Ellen J. Brooks, *Learning to Read and Write: The Role of Language Acquisition and Aesthetic Development* (New York: Garland, 1986), 81–82.

8. Ibid., 90.

9. See for example, Arthur N. Applebee, *The Child's Concept of Story: Ages Two to Seventeen* (Chicago: University of Chicago Press, 1978); Vivian Gussin Paley, *Wally's Stories* (Cambridge, Mass.: Harvard University Press, 1981).

The wons was a fare
she was pret
she was gentle
she was kind
she lived in a castle
up in the sky.

(Alexis, 6 years old).

It is apparent that Alexis has read or heard many fairy tales. She has taken ("borrowed") from them and made certain elements of them her own. We do not call such borrowings plagiarism because we know that all stories are built from other stories. As the writer Jane Yolen observed, "Stories lean on stories" and "all of us use the stories of the past as we tell our own stories."

Psychologist Lawrence Balter reminds us that young children rely heavily on their sense impressions and that those impressions are colored by their emotions. "In other words," says Balter, "they read meaning into their perceptions....I'm saying that kids learn to read a lot of different things before reading in the conventional sense. They read other people's moods, and they read sensory cues. Kids also recognize relationships between shapes and events. Like noticing that there's a small crack in the sidewalk and it is in front of Mr. Jones' house—for them it's like reading a printed street address."

An 18-month-old girl is delighted with a picture book during a Toddler Open House at a branch of the New York Public Library. Photo credit: David Grossman.

THE COLLECTIONS

Collections to support early childhood services include books for infants and toddlers; nonprint materials—recordings, films, videos, computer software, and realia—for infants and toddlers; and print and nonprint materials on parenting for parents and other child caregivers. The materials for parents and caregivers may include a vertical file of pamphlets, newspaper clippings, and other ephemera about early childhood.

The Children's Collection

Books for Infants and Toddlers

Since the late 1970s, publishers have increasingly recognized the need for quality books for infants and young toddlers and have encouraged authors and illustrators to create for this newly discovered audience. Appropriate books for this age group include board books with simple plots, humor, pleasing sounds, rhythmic language patterns, bright, clear illustrations, and sturdy format. Figure-ground contrast with emphasis on the figure, and pictures of familiar objects and events help focus young children's attention.

Safety is another important consideration because infants explore their world by touching, feeling, smelling, and chewing on objects that attract their attention. Cloth books and books made of laminated cardboard with rounded edges, free of toxic substances (or small parts that can come loose), are appropriate. Librarians prefer board books because they are more easily cleaned and shelved, but may want to stock a few quality cloth books as examples to show parents.

Burton White asserts that from about eight or nine months children love books, but what they love about books is the opportunity to practice hand-eye skills. "So, frankly," says White, "one of the two best reasons for getting a book for a one-year-old is to get a book with stiff cardboard pages and the kind of binding that will enable him to struggle—but not too hard—with separating the pages, putting them together, turning the book over, and so forth ad infinitum....I don't mean to trivialize this. My sense (although I can't prove it) is that anything that babies truly enjoy doing with materials is probably educationally beneficial."

The second use for a book, says White, is for labeling sessions. He believes the best books, so far as he can tell from observing young children, are books with single types of subject matter on each page, such as Tana Hoban's *What Is It?*

Children from eighteen months on, or even earlier, are ready for books with a storyline. "You've got to have enough intellectual ability to sustain the interest in a continuing theme and it just isn't there with very many children under twelve months," says White. Not only is the eighteen- to twenty-month-old child intellectually ready, White continues, "but now conspiring to make this a wonderful opportunity is the fact that in the second year of life and sometimes on into the middle of the third year, the strongest goal in any daytime waking child's agenda is winding up the intense relationship between at least one older person and themselves. In the service of completing the first love affair in a human's life, that early attachment process intensifies in the second half of the second year and brings along with it peculiar behaviors like negativism (no, mine) and testing of authority. This is an extremely rich social period of life. One of the almost invariable consequences is a very strong urge for the child to be close to the parent for many hours every day."

There are few activities more pleasurable at this stage of a child's life than cuddling up to a beloved parent and being read to. Toddlers are ready for picture books with a longer storyline, but they still enjoy rhythm, repetition, and rhyme. Choose books with high literary and visual qualities and with subjects of interest. Books for young toddlers should be "attention-grabbing," says Chris Behrmann, children's literature specialist at the New York Public Library.

> Children of this age are fascinated with the exploration of the world around them. The "here and now" is important to them as they begin the process of speaking and responding. Everything attracts their attention, but not for long, as the world is full of things to see, experience, and know about. Picture books with a simple story involving familiar objects or events, and that invite the child to respond in some way, are favorites. Older toddlers, while still interested in books to which they can respond actively, are beginning to enjoy stories which stretch their imaginations and use unusual language. Children this age are learning to anticipate the results of actions before they occur; they are beginning to observe as well as see, picking up details and making inferences from this process. Consequently, the illustrations in their books can be more detailed and the language more sophisticated. Nursery tales with simple plots emphasizing cause and effect, such as "The Three Billy Goats Gruff," are appreciated.

A bibliography of 200 favorites, arranged by developmental stages, follows.

Mother Goose, Poetry, Songs, and Finger Rhymes

Aliki. *Hush, Little Baby*. New York: Prentice-Hall, 1968.

Briggs, Raymond. *The Mother Goose Treasury*. New York: Coward, 1966.

Brown, Marc. *Hand Rhymes*. New York: Dutton, 1985. (See also *Party Rhymes*. (New York: Dutton, 1988.)

Chorao, Kay. *The Baby's Lap Book*. New York: Dutton, 1977, 1990. (See also *The Baby's Bedtime Book* [Doubleday, 1984] and *The Baby's Good Morning Book* [Doubleday, 1986].)

Christelow, Eileen. *Five Little Monkeys Jumping on the Bed*. New York: Clarion, 1989.

Cousins, Lucy, illus. *The Little Dog Laughed and Other Nursery Rhymes*. New York: Dutton, 1990.

de Paola, Tomie. *Tomie de Paola's Mother Goose*. New York: Putnam, 1985.

de Regniers, Beatrice, Eva Moore, Mary Michaels White, and Jan Carr, eds. *Sing a Song of Popcorn: Every Child's Book of Poems*. Illustrated by Marcia Brown, Leo and Diane Dillon, Richard Egielski, Trina Schart Hyman, Arnold Lobel, Maurice Sendak, Marc Simont, and Margot Zemach. New York: Scholastic, 1988.

Duncan, Lois. *Songs from Dreamland*. Illustrated by Kay Chorao. New York: Knopf, 1989.

Ginsburg, Mirra. *The Sun's Asleep Behind the Hill*. Illustrated by Paul O. Zelinsky. New York: Greenwillow, 1982.

Glazer, Tom. *Music for Ones and Twos: Songs and Games for the Very Young Child*. New York: Doubleday, 1983. (See also *Eye Winker, Tom Tinker, Chin Chopper: A Collection of Musical Fingerplays* [Doubleday, 1978].)

Griego, Margot C., et al. *Tortillitas Para Mama: And Other Spanish Nursery Rhymes*. Illustrated by Barbara Cooney. New York: Holt, 1981.

Hart, Jane, ed. *Singing Bee! A Collection of Favorite Children's Songs*. Illustrated by Anita Lobel. New York: Lothrop, 1982.

Hennessy, Barbara G. *A,B,C,D, Tummy, Toes, Hands, Knees*. Illustrated by Wendy Watson. New York: Viking, 1989.

Hopkins, Lee Bennett. *Still as a Star: A Book of Nighttime Poems*. Illustrated by Karen Milone. Boston: Little, Brown, 1989.

Hughes, Shirley. *Out and About*. New York: Lothrop, 1988.

Jeffers, Susan. *All the Pretty Horses*. New York: Scholastic, 1985.

Lamont, Priscilla. *Ring-a-Round-a-Rosy: Nursery Rhymes, Action Rhymes, and Lullabies*. Boston: Little, Brown, 1990.

Larrick, Nancy. *Songs from Mother Goose*. Illustrated by Robin Spart. New York: Harper, 1989. (See also *When the Dark Comes Dancing: A Bedtime Poetry Book* [Philomel, 1983].)

Lobel, Arnold. *The Random House Book of Mother Goose*. New York: Random House, 1986.

Opie, Iona, and Peter Opie. *Tail Feathers from Mother Goose: The Opie Rhyme Book*. Boston: Little, Brown, 1988.

Palmer, Hap. *Baby Songs: A Collection of Songs for the Very Young*. Illustrated by Susannah Ryan. New York: Crown, 1990.

Plotz, Helen. *A Week of Lullabies*. Illustrated by Marisabina Russo. New York: Lothrop, 1988.

Prelutsky, Jack. *Read-Aloud Rhymes for the Very Young*. Illustrated by Marc Brown, with an introduction by Jim Trelease. New York: Knopf, 1986.

Ra, Carol. *Trot Trot to Boston: Play Rhymes for Baby*. Illustrated by Catherine Stock. New York: Lothrop, 1987.

Raffi. *The Raffi Singable Songbook*. New York: Crown, 1980.

Sharon, Lois & Bram's Mother Goose. Illustrated by Maryann Kovalski. Boston: Little, Brown, 1985.

Watson, Wendy. *Wendy Watson's Mother Goose*. New York: Lothrop, 1989.

Weiss, Nicki. *If You're Happy and You Know It*. New York: Greenwillow, 1987.

Yolen, Jane, ed. *The Lap-Time Song and Play Book*. Illustrated by Margot Tomas. San Diego: Harcourt, 1989.

Books for Young Infants

For babies from birth to about seven months—or about babies, to share with older children.

Aliki. *Welcome, Little Baby*. New York: Greenwillow, 1987.

Banish, Roslyn. *Let Me Tell You about My Baby*. New York: Harper, 1982.

Burningham, John. *The Baby*. New York: Crowell, 1975.

Cuyler, Margery. *Shadow's Baby*. Illustrated by Ellen Weiss. New York: Clarion, 1989.

Hello Baby. Photographs by Debby Slier. New York: Macmillan, 1988.

Henderson, Kathy. *The Baby's Book of Babies*. Photographs by Anthea Sieveking. New York: Dial, 1988.

Hoffman, Phyllis. *Baby's First Year*. Illustrated by Sarah Wilson. New York: Lippincott, 1988.

Jonas, Ann. *When You Were a Baby*. New York: Morrow, 1982 (available in boards, Sept. 1991).

Keats, Ezra Jack. *Peter's Chair*. New York: Viking, 1967.

Lasky, Kathryn. *A Baby for Max*. Photographs by Christopher G. Knight. New York: Scribners, 1984.

Ormerod, Jan. *101 Things to Do with a Baby*. New York: Puffin/Penguin, 1984.

Patent, Dorothy Hinshaw. *Babies!* New York: Holiday House, 1988.

Rojankovsky, Feodor. *Animals on the Farm*. New York: Knopf, 1967.

Sage, Angie, and Chris Sage. *Happy Baby*. New York: Dial, 1990. (See other titles in this series.)

Scott, Ann Herbert. *On Mother's Lap*. Drawings by Glo Coalson. New York: McGraw-Hill, 1972.

Voake, Charlotte. *First Things First. A Baby's Companion—ABC, 1 2 3, Rhymes and Pictures.* Boston: Little, Brown, 1988.

Williams, Garth. *Baby Farm Animals.* New York: Western/Golden Book, 1983.

Williams, Susan. *Poppy's First Year.* New York: Four Winds, 1989.

Willis, Jeanne. *Earthlets as Explained by Professor Xargle.* Illustrated by Tony Ross. New York: Dutton, 1989.

Books for Older Infants

For babies from about seven to fourteen months.

Ahlberg, Janet, and Allan Ahlberg. *The Baby's Catalogue.* Boston: Little, Brown/Atlantic Monthly, 1983. (See also *Peek-a-Boo* [Viking, 1981].)

Brown, Margaret Wise. *Goodnight Moon.* Illustrated by Clement Hurd. New York: Harper, 1947. (Available in boards, Sept. 1991.)

Burningham, John. *The Blanket.* New York: Crowell, 1976. (*The Baby, The Dog, The Rabbit, The Friend, The School, The Snow,* and *The Cupboard* are other titles in this series.)

Chen, Tony. *Wild Animals.* New York: Random House, 1981.

Fujikawa, Gyo. *Gyo Fujikawa's A to Z Picture Book.* New York: Grosset, 1974. (See also *Baby Animals* [Grosset, 1963].)

Gäg, Wanda. *The ABC Bunny.* New York: Coward, McCann, 1933.

Gillham, Bill. *The First Words Picture Book.* New York: Coward, McCann, 1982.

Hayes, Sarah. *Eat Up, Gemma.* Illustrated by Jan Ormerod. New York: Lothrop, 1988.

Hoban, Tana. *What Is It?* New York: Greenwillow, 1985. (See also *1, 2, 3* [Greenwillow, 1985] and *Red, Blue, Yellow Shoe* [Greenwillow, 1986].)

Kamen, Gloria. *''Paddle,'' Said the Swan.* New York: Atheneum, 1989.

Kunhardt, Dorothy. *Pat the Bunny.* New York: Golden Books, 1942.

Leonard, Marcia. *What I Like* series: *Eating, Getting Dressed, Going to Bed,* and *Taking a Bath.* Illustrated by Deborah Michel. New York: Bantam, 1988.

MacKinnon, Debbie. *Ten Little Babies.* Illustrated by Lisa Kopper. New York: Dutton, 1990.

McMillan, Bruce. *Step by Step.* New York: Lothrop, 1987.

Ormerod, Jan. *The Saucepan Game.* New York: Lothrop, 1989. (Also see Ormerod's Baby Books series, including *Dad's Back, Messy Baby, Reading,* and *Sleeping.*)

Oxenbury, Helen. *Clap Hands.* New York: Aladdin, 1987. (Other titles in this series are *All Fall Down, Say Goodnight,* and *Tickle, Tickle.* See also Helen Oxenbury's Baby Board Books: *Dressing, Family, Friends, Playing,* and *Working.* New York: Simon & Schuster, 1981.)

Polushkin, Maria. *Who Said Meow?* Illustrated by Ellen Weiss. New York: Bradbury, 1988.

Rice, Eve. *What Sadie Sang*. New York: Greenwillow, 1976. (Issued in a new, larger format in 1983.)

Tafuri, Nancy. *The Ball Bounced*. New York: Greenwillow, 1989. (See also Nancy Tafuri's Board Books: *In a Red House, My Friends*, and *Where We Sleep* [Greenwillow, 1987].)

Watanabe, Shigeo. *Daddy, Play with Me!* Illustrated by Yasuo Ohtomo. New York: Philomel, 1985. (See other titles in the "I Love to Do Things with Daddy" series.)

Williams, Vera B. *"More More More," Said the Baby: 3 Love Stories*. New York: Greenwillow, 1990.

Wright, Blanche Fisher. *The Real Mother Goose*. Chicago: Rand McNally, 1983. (Husky Books 1 and 2.)

Zolotow, Charlotte. *Sleepy Book*. New York: Harper, 1988.

Books for Young Toddlers

For toddlers from about fifteen to twenty-four months.

Ahlberg, Janet, and Allan Ahlberg. *Each Peach Pear Plum*. New York: Viking, 1979.

Bang, Molly. *Ten, Nine, Eight*. New York: Greenwillow, 1983.

Barton, Bryon. *Airport*. New York: Crowell, 1982.

Brown, Margaret Wise. *The Runaway Bunny*. Illustrated by Clement Hurd. New York: Harper, 1972. (See also *Big Red Barn*, illustrated by Felicia Bond [Harper, 1989].)

Burningham, John. *Mr. Gumpy's Motor Car*. New York: Crowell, 1976. (See also *Mr. Gumpy's Outing* [Holt, 1971].)

Butler, Dorothy. *My Brown Bear Barney*. Illustrated by Elizabeth Fuller. New York: Greenwillow, 1989.

Campbell, Rod. *Dear Zoo*. New York: Four Winds Press, 1983.

Carle, Eric. *The Very Hungry Caterpillar*. New York: Putnam, 1981.

Cazet, Denys. *Mother Night*. New York: Orchard Books, 1989.

Crews, Donald. *Freight Train*. New York: Greenwillow, 1978. (See also *Truck* [Greenwillow, 1980] and *Flying* [Greenwillow, 1986].)

Galdone, Paul. *The Gingerbread Boy*. New York: Clarion, 1983.

Ginsburg, Mirra. *Good Morning, Chick*. Illustrated by Bryon Barton. New York: Greenwillow, 1980.

Guy, Ginger Foglesong. *Black Crow, Black Crow*. Illustrated by Nancy Parker. New York: Greenwillow, 1991.

Hill, Erik. *Where's Spot?* New York: Putnam, 1980. (All stories about this popular dog are now available in Spanish.)

Hughes, Shirley. *Two Shoes, New Shoes*. New York: Lothrop, 1986. (Other titles in the Shirley Hughes Nursery Collection are *Bathwater's Hot, Noisy, When We Went to the Park, Colors*, and *All Shapes and Sizes*.)

Isadora, Rachel. *I Touch*. New York: Greenwillow, 1985. (See also *I See* [Greenwillow, 1985]. Both available in boards, Sept. 1991.)

Lindgren, Barbro. *Sam's Bath*. New York: Morrow, 1983. (See other books in this series.)

Lloyd, David. *Duck*. New York: Lippincott, 1988.

Maris, Ron. *Are You There, Bear?* New York: Greenwillow, 1985.

Martin, Bill, Jr., and John Archambault. *Listen to the Rain*. Illustrated by James Endicott. New York: Holt, 1988.

Ormerod, Jan. *Moonlight*. New York: Lothrop, 1982. (*Sunshine* is a companion book.)

Porter-Gaylord, Laurel. *I Love My Daddy Because...* and *I Love My Mommy Because....* Illustrated by Ashley Wolff. New York: Dutton, 1991.

Rice, Eve. *Goodnight, Goodnight*. New York: Greenwillow, 1980.

Rockwell, Anne. *In Our House*. New York: Crowell, 1985.

Shannon, George. *Oh, I Love*. Illustrated by Cheryl Harness. New York: Bradbury, 1988.

Shaw, Charles. *It Looked Like Spilt Milk*. New York: Harper, 1947.

Spier, Peter. *Crash! Bang! Boom!* New York: Doubleday, 1972. (See also *Gobble, Growl, Grunt* [Doubleday, 1971].)

Steptoe, John. *Baby Says*. New York: Lothrop, 1988.

Stickland, Paul. *A Child's Book of Things*. New York: Orchard Books, 1990.

Tafuri, Nancy. *Have You Seen My Duckling?* New York: Greenwillow, 1984.

Vincent, Gabrielle. *Ernest and Celestine's Picnic*. New York: Greenwillow, 1982. (See also other stories about this lovable bear and his mouse friend.)

Wells, Rosemary. *Max's Ride*. New York: Dial, 1979. (See other stories about Max and his sister Ruby.)

Wheeler, Cindy. *A Good Day, A Good Night*. New York: Lippincott, 1980. (See also other stories about Marmalade the cat introduced in this title.)

Whiteside, Karen. *Lullaby of the Wind*. Illustrated by Kazue Mizumura. New York: Harper, 1984.

Ziefert, Harriet. *Daddy, Can You Play with Me?* and *Mommy, Where Are You?* Illustrated by Emilie Boon. New York: Viking, 1988.

_____, and Arnold Lobel. *Where's Cat?* New York: Harper, 1987. (See also *Bear Gets Dressed* [Harper, 1986].)

Books for Older Toddlers

For toddlers from about twenty-five to thirty-six months.

Anno, Mitsumasa. *Anno's Counting House*. New York: Philomel, 1982.

Argent, Kerry. *Animal Capers*. New York: Dial, 1986.

Arnosky, Jim. *Watching Foxes*. New York: Lothrop, 1985.

Asch, Frank. *Happy Birthday, Moon*. Englewood Cliffs, N.J.: Prentice-Hall, 1982. (See also *Just Like Daddy* [Prentice-Hall, 1981].)

Bang, Molly. *Yellow Ball*. New York: Greenwillow, 1991.

Banks, Merry. *Animals of the Night*. Illustrated by Ronald Himler. New York: Scribners, 1990.

Bemelmans, Ludwig. *Madeline*. New York: Viking, 1939, 1967.

Bornstein, Ruth. *Little Gorilla*. New York: Clarion, 1986.

Brett, Jan. *Goldilocks and the Three Bears*. New York: Dodd, Mead, 1987.

Briggs, Raymond. *The Snowman*. New York: Random House, 1978.

Brown, Marcia. *The Three Billy Goats Gruff*. New York: Harcourt, 1957.

de Brunhoff, Jean. *The Story of Babar*. New York: Random House, 1937.

Degan, Bruce. *Jamberry*. New York: Harper, 1983.

Ehlert, Lois. *Color Zoo*. New York: Lippincott, 1989.

Field, Rachel. *General Store*. Illustrated by Giles Laroche. Boston: Little, Brown, 1988.

Freeman, Don. *Corduroy*. New York: Viking, 1960.

Hoban, Tana. *Of Colors and Things*. New York: Greenwillow, 1989. (See also *Push Pull, Empty Full: A Book of Opposites* [Macmillan, 1972] and other concept books by this talented photographer and author.)

Hughes, Shirley. *Alfie Gets in First*. New York: Lothrop, 1982. (See other stories about Alfie.)

Hutchins, Pat. *Changes, Changes*. New York: Macmillan, 1971. (See also *Rosie's Walk* [Macmillan, 1968].)

Jacobs, Joseph. *The Three Little Pigs*. Illustrated by Erik Blegvad. New York: Atheneum, 1980.

Johnson, Angela. *When I Am Old with You*. Illustrated by David Soman. New York: Orchard Books, 1990.

Keats, Ezra Jack. *The Snowy Day*. New York: Viking, 1962. (See other stories about Peter and his friends.)

Kitchen, Bert. *Animal Alphabet*. New York: Dial, 1984. (See also the companion volume *Animal Numbers* [Dial, 1984].)

Krauss, Ruth. *A Very Special House*. Illustrated by Maurice Sendak. New York: Harper, 1953.

Le Tord, Bijou. *A Brown Cow*. Boston: Little, Brown, 1989. (See also *The Deep Blue Sea* [Orchard Books, 1990].)

Lobel, Arnold, *Frog and Toad Are Friends*. New York: Harper, 1972. (See other titles in this series.)

Lyon, George Ella. *Basket*. Illustrated by Mary Szilagyi. New York: Orchard Books, 1990.

MacDonald, Suse. *Alphabatics*. New York: Bradbury, 1986.

McMillan, Bruce. *Kitten Can . . . .* New York: Lothrop, 1984.

McPhail, David. *Emma's Pet*. New York: Dutton, 1985.

Martin, Bill, Jr. *Brown Bear, Brown Bear, What Do You See?* Illustrated by Eric Carle. New York: Holt, 1983.

Marzollo, Jean. *Pretend You're a Cat*. Illustrated by Jerry Pinkney. New York: Dial, 1990.

Oxenbury, Helen. *Tom and Pippo Read a Story*. New York: Aladdin, 1988. (See other stories about Tom and Pippo.)

Peek, Merle. *Mary Wore a Red Dress and Henry Wore His Green Sneakers*. New York: Clarion, 1985.

Potter, Beatrix. *The Tale of Peter Rabbit*. New York: Viking, 1987. (See other animal tales by this classic author and illustrator.)

Pryor, Ainslie. *The Baby Blue Cat and the Smiley Worm Doll*. New York: Viking, 1990. (Other titles in this series are *The Baby Blue Cat Who Said No*, *The Baby Blue Cat and the Whole Batch of Cookies*, *The Baby Blue Cat and the Dirty Dog Brothers*.)

Rockwell, Anne and Harlow Rockwell. *The Tool Box*. Illustrated by Harlow Rockwell. New York: Macmillan, 1971.

Rosen, Michael. *We're Going on a Bear Hunt*. Illustrated by Helen Oxenbury. New York: McElderry Books, 1989.

Sendak, Maurice. *Where the Wild Things Are*. New York: Harper, 1963.

Serfozo, Mary. *Who Said Red?* Illustrated by Keiko Narahashi. New York: Atheneum/McElderry, 1988.

Sis, Peter. *Beach Ball*. New York: Greenwillow, 1990. (See also *Going Up* [Greenwillow, 1989].)

Tafuri, Nancy. *Follow Me*. New York: Greenwillow, 1990.

Tolstoy, Alexei. *The Great Big Enormous Turnip*. Illustrated by Helen Oxenbury. New York: Franklin Watts, 1969.

Vipont, Elfrida. *The Elephant and the Bad Baby*. Illustrated by Raymond Briggs. New York: Coward, McCann, 1969.

Waddell, Martin. *Can't You Sleep, Little Bear?* Illustrated by Barbara Firth. London: Walker, 1988.

Watanabe, Shigeo. *How Do I Put It On?* Illustrated by Yasuo Ohtomo. New York: Philomel, 1977. (See other titles in the "I Can Do It All by Myself" series.)

Yashima, Taro. *Umbrella*. New York: Viking, 1958.

Young, Ed. *Up a Tree*. New York: Harper, 1983.

Nonprint Materials for Infants and Toddlers

Musical Recordings   Babies are born with the ability to hear. In fact, unborn babies are known to become more active in the womb when subjected to loud sounds. The newborn seems to prefer human voices and especially her mother's voice. The best musical recordings for infants and young toddlers are attention-getting without being startling or intrusive. Babies enjoy lullabies, bouncing and action rhymes, songs that invite finger and toe play, and songs about everyday activities. Toddlers enjoy swaying to music, marching to spirited rhythms, and singing along to catchy verses. Recordings by Tom Glazer, Ella Jenkins, Hap Palmer, and Raffi are good choices. Collections need not be limited to recordings made especially for infants and toddlers. Librarians should encourage parents to introduce whatever types of music they enjoy, including some classical, jazz, ethnic, folk, and religious music. Even very young children respond with pleasure to selections from Haydn and Mozart, Humperdinck and Sousa. By hearing a variety of types of music in early childhood, children open themselves to the entire world of music. And just as children learn language naturally by

Listening to records at the Saratoga Springs (N.Y.) Public Library. Photo credit: Ellen deLalla.

hearing it spoken, so they learn to distinguish instruments and to identify melody, harmony, and rhythm naturally when music is part of their everyday environment.

A selected list of musical recordings follows.

Musical Recordings

All Through the Night. Performed by Diane Green. Caedmon CAE 1843 (cassette).

American Folk Songs for Children. Sung by Pete Seeger. Smithsonian/ Folkways SF 45020 (record/cassette).

Animal Crackers and Other Tasty Tunes. Sung by Kevin Roth. CMS Records/Alcazar 706 (record/cassette).

Babes, Beasts, and Birds. Featuring Pat Carfra. Lullaby Lady Productions/ distributed by Alcazar JOL 3 (record/cassette). ALA Notable Children's Recording 1988.

Baby and Me: Playsongs and Lullabies to Share with Your Baby. Sung by Rachael Buchman. A Gentle Wind GW 1055 (cassette).

Baby Face: Activities for Infants and Toddlers. Kimbo Educational Records KIM 7049/7049c (record/cassette).

The Baby Record. Performed by Bob McGrath and Katharine Smithrim. Kids' Records KRL 100KRC 1007 (record/cassette).

Baby's Bedtime. Lullabies from Kay Chorao's book, sung by Judy Collins. Lightyear Entertainment/Records LIGHT-5102 (cassette). Other titles in this series include *Baby's Morningtime,* sung by Judy Collins, LIGHT-5104; *Baby's Nursery Rhymes,* sung by Phylicia Rashad, LIGHT-5107.

BabySong. By Hap and Martha Palmer. Educational Activities AR 713/AC 713 (record/cassette). ALA Notable Children's Recording 1985.

Bean Bag Activities. Kimbo Educational Records KIM 7055/7055c (record/cassette).

Birds, Beasts, Bugs and Little Fishes. Sung by Pete Seeger. Smithsonian/ Folkways SF 45021 (cassette).

Camels, Cats and Rainbows. Sung by Paul Strausman. A Gentle Wind GW 1009 (Cassette). ALA Notable Children's Recording 1983.

A Child's Gift of Lullabies. By J. Aaron Brown & Associates. Featuring Tanya Goodman. JAB 52221 (cassette). Available in Spanish under the title *Un Regalo de Arullos,* JAB 52222. ALA Notable Children's Recording 1989.

Did You Feed My Cow? Fred Koch and a group of children present the songs of Ella Jenkins. Red Rover Records RRR-333 (record/cassette).

Early, Early Childhood Songs. Featuring Ella Jenkins. Smithsonian/ Folkways SF 45015 (record/cassette). See other recordings by this well-loved performer.

Earth Mother Lullabies from Around the World. Vols. 1 and 2. Featuring Pamela Ballingham backed by harp, flute, mandolin, guitar, and percussion instruments. Earth Mother Productions EMIA/EMP 02B (2 cassettes). ALA Notable Children's Recordings 1986, 1988.

Everything Grows. Featuring Raffi. MCA 10039 (record/cassette). ALA Notable Children's Recording 1988. (Raffi's earlier recordings *Singable Songs for the Very Young* and *More Singable Songs for the Very Young* [MCA 10037 and MCA 10038] continue to be toddler favorites.)

Favorite Marches. Performed by Arthur Fiedler and the Boston Pops. RCA Records RK 5071 (record/cassette).

Golden Slumbers: Lullabies from Near and Far. Performed by Oscar Brand, Jean Ritchie, Pete Seeger, and other folksingers. Caedmon CAE 1399 (cassette).

Good Morning Sunshine. Featuring Patti Dallas and Laura Baron. Golden Glow Recordings/distributed by Alcazar GOLD 102 (cassette).

Haydn: Symphony No. 94 in G ("Surprise"). Performed by the London Philharmonic Orchestra conducted by Georg Solti. London LON 41897-4 (cassette).

Hello Everybody! Playsongs and Rhymes from a Toddler's World. Sung by Rachael Buchman. A Gentle Wind GW 1038 (cassette). ALA Notable Children's Recording 1987.

Humperdinck: *Evening Prayer* from *Hansel and Gretel*, Act 2. Performed by the New York Philharmonic conducted by Leonard Bernstein. Columbia COL MLK-44723 (cassette).

If You're Happy and You Know It Sing Along with Bob. Vols. 1 and 2. Sung by Sesame Street's Bob McGrath. Kids' Records KRL/KRC 1009 and KRL/KRC 1014 (2 records/cassettes).

It's Toddler Time. Featuring Carol Hammett. Kimbo Educational Records KIM 0815/0815c (record/cassette).

Jump Children. Sung by Marcy Marxer. Rounder Records RDR 8012 (record/ cassette).

Let's Sing Fingerplays. Tom Glazer sings fourteen selections from the book *Eye Winker, Tom Tinker, Chin Chopper: Fifty Musical Fingerplays.* CMS Records CMS 688/CMS X4688 (record/cassette).

Little Hands: Songs for and about Children. American Melody AM 102/ AMC 102 (record/cassette). ALA Notable Children's Recording 1986.

Lullabies for Little Dreamers. Kevin Roth accompanies himself on the mountain dulcimer. CMS Records CMS 696/CMS X4696 (record/ cassette).

Lullabies Go Jazz: Sweet Sounds for Sweet Dreams. By Jon Crosse. Jazz Cat Productions JCR 101/JCC101 (record/cassette). ALA Notable Children's Recording 1987.

Mail Myself to You. Featuring John McCutcheon accompanied by children, hammer dulcimer, and ham bone. Rounder Records RDR 8016 (record/cassette). ALA Notable Children's Recording 1989.

Mainly Mother Goose; Songs and Rhymes for Merry Young Souls. Performed by Sharon, Lois & Bram. Elephant Records EF 301 (record/cassette). ALA Notable Children's Recording 1985. (See other tapes by this popular trio from Canada.)

Marcia Berman Sings Lullabies and Songs You Never Dreamed Were Lullabies. B/B Records BB/BBC 113 (record/cassette).

Mozart. *Eine Kleine Nachtmusik.* Performed by Eugene Ormandy and the Philadelphia Orchestra. Columbia COL 39436 (cassette).

Music for Ones and Twos: Songs & Games for Young Children and *More Music for Ones and Twos.* Sung by Tom Glazer. CMS Records CMS 649/CMS X4649 and CMS 697/CMS X4697 (2 records/cassettes).

Nitey-Nite. Featuring Patti Dallas and Laura Baron. Golden Glow Recordings/distributed by Alcazar GOLD 101 (cassette).

Prokofiev. *Peter and the Wolf.* Performed by the New York Philharmonic with Leonard Bernstein conducting and narrating. Reverse: Tchaikovsky's *Nutcracker Suite.* Columbia COL MY 37765 (cassette).

Saint-Saens. *Carnival of Animals.* Performed by the New York Philharmonic conducted by Leonard Bernstein. Reverse: *The Sorcerer's Apprentice.* Columbia COL 39018 (cassette).

The Sandman: Lullabies and Night Time Songs. Sung by Kevin Roth and Grant Birchard. Marlboro Records MARL 005 (cassette). ALA Notable Children's Recording 1989.

Sleepytime Serenade. Sung by Linda Schrade accompanied by guitar and flute music. A Gentle Wind GW 1048 (cassette).

Songs & Games for Toddlers. Performed by Bob McGrath and Katharine Smithrim with percussion by Bill Usher. Kids' Records KRL/KRC 1016 (record/cassette).

Songs and Playtime. Sung by Pete Seeger. Smithsonian/Folkways SF 45023 (cassette).

Songs for Sleepyheads and Out-of-Beds. Featuring Pat Carfra. Lullaby Lady Productions/distributed by Alcazar JOL5 (record/cassette).

Songs from Dreamland: Original Lullabies by Lois Duncan. Sung by Robin Arquette. Accompanied by book illustrated by Kay Chorao. Random House 0-394-82862-3 (cassette).

Songs to Grow on for Mother and Child. Sung by Woody Guthrie. Smithsonian/Folkways SF 45035 (cassette).

Sousa. *Sousa Marches in Hi-Fi*. Performed by the Goldman Band. MCA Distributing Corp. MCA C-4 (cassette).

Star Dreamer: Nightsongs and Lullabies. Sung by Priscilla Herdman and Abby Newton. Alcazar Records ALA 1001/ALA 1001c (record/cassette). ALA Notable Children's Recording 1989.

Strauss. *Johann Strauss' Greatest Hits*. Performed by the Philadelphia Orchestra conducted by Eugene Ormandy. Columbia COL MLK-39432 (cassette).

Tickly Toddle: Songs for Very Young Children. Sung by Hap Palmer. Educational Activities AR597/AC597 (record/cassette).

Toddlers on Parade. Kimbo Educational Records KIM 9002/9002c (record/cassette).

Turkey in the Straw: Bluegrass Songs for Children. Featuring Phil Rosenthal. American Melody Records AM 101 (record).

Films and Videos

Maureen Gaffney, the founder and executive director of the Center for Children's Media, which provides the public with research-based information about using educational films and videos with children ages two to fourteen, notes that television viewing has made toddlers and preschoolers visually sophisticated. Quality films for young children have been available for many years; however, the video medium has not caught up yet. Most of the better videos are films based on distinguished picture books that have been transferred to the video medium.

The main review sources for librarians are *Booklist*, *School Library Journal*, *Parents' Choice*, *Video Librarian*, and *Children's Video Report*. Also check the annual list "Notable Films and Videos for Children," films and videos selected by the Association for Library Service to Children of the American Library Association. An excellent resource to use in staff training or parent education programs is *Choosing the Best in Children's Video*,[1] a 1990 ALA Video hosted by Christopher Reeve. The 35-minute video features Peggy Charren of ACT (Action

1. American Library Association, *Choosing the Best in Children's Video*, 36 min. (Chicago: American Library Association, 1990). Order from ALA Graphics, American Library Association, 50 E. Huron Street, Chicago, IL 60611.

for Children's Television), child development specialists, children's librarians, and children's video producers talking about the criteria for video selection. The tape includes clips from more than thirty outstanding children's videos.

"The best films have atmosphere and texture, and use music, sound, pacing, and lighting to create mood," according to Marilyn Iarusso, chair of the New York Public Library's Children's Film Evaluation Committee and for eighteen years a juror for children's films at the American Film Festival. Iarusso believes film is one of the most powerful communicators because it engages so many of the child's senses. Although she prefers film over video for library film programs due to the superiority of picture quality, the greater impact of a large image in a darkened room, and the pretheater experience it offers children, she lists the following advantages of video over 16mm film: "cost, convenience, simplicity, durability, repeatability, fast forward and freeze frame, and sound quality." I prefer video for toddlers for the intimacy of the small screen. A short list of films and videos suitable for use in programs for toddlers, compiled by Susan Pine and me, can be found at the end of this section. The titles listed meet the following criteria:

eight minutes and under

lively music or sound effects

sense of humor

based on books or realia likely to be in a library collection

familiar subject matter with toddler appeal.

You will also want to purchase longer videos, such as *Young People's Concert with Raffi* (45 mins.; A&M Video), *Meet Your Animal Friends* (54 min.; available from UPBEAT) and *The Snowman* (26 min.; Weston Woods) for the collection.

Short Films and Videos for Toddlers

Caps for Sale. Weston Woods. 5 min. Iconography.

Catsup. Tana Hoban Films/Films, Inc. 3 min. Live action.

Changes, Changes. Weston Woods. 6 min. Animation.

Cheechako's First Day. Encyclopaedia Britannica Educational Corp. 8 min. Live action. (16mm only)

Chicken Soup with Rice. Weston Woods. 5 min. Animation.

Dance Squared. National Film Board of Canada. 4 min. Animation.

41 Barks. Tana Hoban Films/Films, Inc. 1 min. Animation.

Frederick (on *Five Lionni Classics*). Random House. 6 min. Animation.

The Garden (on *Frog and Toad Together*). Churchill Films. 4 min. Puppet animation.

Happy Birthday, Moon. Weston Woods. 7 min. Animation.

Harold and the Purple Crayon. Weston Woods. 8 min. Animation.

Hot Hippo. Weston Woods. 6 min. Animation.

Hush Little Baby. Weston Woods. 5 min. Iconography.

It's Snow. National Film Board of Canada. 6 min. Animation.

Lullaby. Pannonia Films, Budapest. Distributed by International Film Bureau. 3½ min. Animation. (16mm only)

Luxo, Jr. Pixar Animation Production Group/Direct Cinema, Ltd. 3 min. Computer animation.
Madeline's Rescue. Weston Woods. 7 min. Animation.
Matrioska. National Film Board of Canada. 5 min. Animation.
Max's Chocolate Chicken. Weston Woods. 5 min. Animation.
Max's Christmas. Weston Woods. 5 min. Animation.
Mole and the Egg. Phoenix/BFA Films. 6 min. Animation.
Morris's Disappearing Bag. Weston Woods. 6 min. Animation.
One Was Johnny. Weston Woods. 3 min. Animation.
A Rainbow of My Own. Live Oak Media. 5 min. Iconography. (VHS only)
Rosie's Walk. Weston Woods. 5 min. Animation.
Snowy Day. Weston Woods. 6 min. Animation.
Sole Mani. Direct Cinema. 4 min. Live action.
Three Billy Goats Gruff. Weston Woods. 6 min. Iconography. (VHS only)
Whistle for Willie. Weston Woods. 6 min. Animation.
Wynken, Blynken, and Nod. Weston Woods. 4 min. Iconography.

Computer Programs

In their book *The Preschool Years*, Ellen Galinsky and Judy David discuss the pros and cons of computers for preschoolers. Many young children like computers, probably because they enjoy pushing buttons and making images appear on the screen. Galinsky and David cite a research study by early childhood educators Sandra Anselmo and Ann Zinck. Computers and developmentally appropriate software were placed in nursery school classrooms that also had a variety of other materials, such as blocks and paints. The children were shown how to operate the computers and then allowed to use them freely. They were shown how to use software only if they were interested or had questions. The researchers found that the computers promoted skill development in comprehension, memory, evaluation, problem solving, and creativity. Furthermore, cooperation was fostered as the children helped one another and worked together. The researchers concluded that if used in developmentally appropriate ways, computers could stimulate thinking skills.[2]

The arguments against computers in the early years presented by Galinsky and David are:

1. Young children learn best by direct, hands-on experience; computers present abstractions.
2. Computers limit experimentation and flexibility.
3. Some implicit lessons of computers are not beneficial [they require a somewhat inactive, passive orientation].
4. Many software programs are inappropriate for young children: they present drills, are violent, or require too much reading.[3]

2. Sandra Anselmo and R. Ann Zinck, "Computers for Young Children? Perhaps," *Young Children* 42:3 (March 1987): 22–27, quoted in Ellen Galinsky and Judy David, *The Preschool Years* (New York: New York Times Books, 1988), 91.
3. Ibid., 91.

Galinsky and David conclude that "computers are most appropriate for children who are ready to make a transition from relying on actual objects and events to abstract thinking. In Piaget's terms, these are the children who are moving from preoperational to concrete operation thinking....In our opinion, the computer offers no learning experience nor fosters any skill for preschool children that cannot be experienced more meaningful and less expensively in play at home and in good early childhood programs. The value of computers for learning comes later on, when children are older."[4]

Susan Pine and Katherine Todd, two NYPL children's librarians with experience in introducing toddlers to the computer, note that well-designed programs reinforce and build on a child's knowledge as well as teach new skills. They recommend software that offers colorful and recognizable grahics, tuneful music, and sound effects, such as *Charlie Brown's ABC's*, *Muppetville*, and *Stickybear Numbers*. A short list of recommended computer programs for toddlers, compiled by Pine, follows.

Computer Programs for Preschoolers

Charlie Brown's ABC's. American School Publishers. Apple II series; Commodore 64.

Charlie Brown's 1,2,3's. American School Publishers. Apple II series.

Early Games for Young Children. Springboard. Apple II series; Commodore 64; IBM PC; Macintosh.

Easy as ABC. Springboard. Apple II series; Commodore 64; IBM PC; Macintosh.

Juggle's Rainbow. Learning Company. Apple II series.

Kindercomp. Spinnaker. Apple II series; Commodore 64.

Mask Parade. Springboard. Apple II series; IBM PC.

Math and Me. Davidson & Associates, Inc. Apple II series; talking version, Apple IIGS 512K; IBM; Tandy.

Math Rabbit. Learning Company. Apple II Series; IBM; Tandy.

Mr. and Mrs. Potato Head. American School Publishers. Apple II series.

Muppetville. Sunburst. Apple II series (use with Muppet Keyboard).

Muppet Word Book. Sunburst. Apple II series (use with Muppet Keyboard).

Number Farm. DLM Teaching Resources. Apple II series; IBM.

Stickybear ABC. Weekly Reader/Optimum Resources, Inc. Apple II series; Atari; Commodore.

Stickybear Numbers. Weekly Reader/Optimum Resources, Inc. Apple II series; Atari; Commodore.

Stickybear Opposites. Weekly Reader/Optimum Resources, Inc. Apple II series; Atari; Commodore.

4. Ibid., 93.

Realia

The library, by providing realia—such as toys, puzzles, games, puppets, musical instruments, costumes, props, and so on—that can be manipulated and explored in play, becomes a relevant place for children who are at Piaget's concrete stage of development. Through play, children develop motor skills, eye-hand coordination, and perceptual skills such as perceptual-motor, spatial, figure-ground, whole-part, classification, sequence, and clue awareness. These skills form the basis for learning to read. Other valid reasons for including realia in the library are (1) to help parents and caregivers understand play as a mode of learning, (2) to give parents an opporunity to observe how their children interact with different toys before making home purchases, and (3) to meet the needs of parents and early childhood professionals for information on selecting toys for children at different stages of development. With so much television advertising of expensive toys, parents and other child caregivers may need to be reminded that simple hand-made toys have play value. *Toys to Grow With! Infants and Toddlers*, by John Fisher, co-creator of Johnson & Johnson Development Toys, includes directions for fifty toys that can be easily made; among them are crib mobiles, texture books, sock bean bags, giant grocery bag blocks (made from brown paper grocery bags stuffed with crumpled newspapers and taped closed), and people puzzles made from family photographs.[5]

Criteria for Choosing Toys

The criteria for toy selection include safety, durability, child appeal (or play value), aesthetic value, and teaching and learning potential.

Safety. Toys for the library collection should be sturdy; washable or easily cleaned; large enough so they cannot be swallowed; and free of sharp edges, small detachable parts, or parts that may pinch or clamp children. For children under the age of three, no toy or piece of toy should be smaller than one and a quarter inches in diameter and two and a quarter inches in depth. Smaller items can become lodged in the windpipe, ears, or nostrils. Cords or strings, if any, should be no longer than twelve inches. Painted toys should carry a "nontoxic" label, and fabrics a "nonflammable" label. The United States Consumer Product Safety Commission has been active in this area and has published *Which Toy for Which Child: A Consumer's Guide for Selecting Suitable Toys Ages Birth through Five.*[6]

Durability. "A good toy should be able to withstand fingering, mouthing, banging, hammering, and occasionally being stepped on without falling apart," according to Barbara Kaban, author of *Choosing Toys for Children from Birth to Five.*[7] Before purchasing a toy for the library collection, librarians

---

5. John J. Fisher, *Toys to Grow With! Infants and Toddlers* (New York: Putnam, 1986).
6. For a free copy, write to the Office of Information and Public Affairs, U.S. Consumer Products Safety Commission, 5401 Westbard Avenue, Bethesda, MD 20207.
7. Barbara Kaban, *Choosing Toys for Children from Birth to Five* (New York: Schocken, 1979), 2.

Parents and children in the Toy Center, Westbury Memorial Public Library. Photo provided by the library, which is part of the Nassau Library System, Uniondale, New York.

should consider the quality of its construction, whether it is repairable, and whether the library has adequate storage space to reduce the possibility of breakage. Librarians will need to check the condition of each item regularly for any needed repairs or missing pieces.

Child appeal, or play value. It has been said that the ideal toy is 90 percent child and 10 percent toy; that is, a good toy stimulates the child's imagination and invites effort. In *Toys to Go,* Jean Rustici, early childhood education consultant at the Connecticut Department of Education, recommends toys that "give [the child] opportunity to return to an object many times to explore various play possibilities with it at several different levels of development."[8]

Aesthetic value. Toys should be well designed—pleasing in line, color, proportion, and general appearance. They should be pleasant to hold, and in the case of musical toys, pleasing to the ear.

Teaching and learning potential. There are toys that encourage active physical play, toys that encourage thinking or cognitive skills, toys that encourage social skills, and toys that encourage creativity or expression of feelings. But, as Kaban reminds her readers, "Most toys encompass more than one skill or ability." In figure 3, you will find a chart of toys and activities for young children.

When purchasing toys for the library collection, think in terms of connecting some with books. A book such as Tana Hoban's *Circles, Triangles, and Squares,* for instance, is a natural lead-in to play with shape sorters. A toddler, after listening to *Where's Spot?*, might use the stuffed animal Spot to imagine further adventures with the lovable puppy.

Sources for Purchasing Toys

Buy Me! Buy Me! The Bank Street Guide to Choosing Toys for Children, by Joanne Oppenheim, is an excellent guide to choosing the best toys from among the multitude of commercial toys on the market.[9] It is profusely illustrated with photographs of many of the items cited in the text. To see toys, visit the toy sections of local department stores and large discount houses, such as Toys 'Я' Us, and attend toy fairs whenever possible.

Catalogs from toy manufacturers can help you compare prices of similar items and learn about new items. Ask to be placed on the mailing lists of reputable toy manufacturers or suppliers, such as the ones listed on page 69. When looking for a particular toy without success, write directly to the manufacturer. The following addresses may be helpful:

Ambi
Davis-Grabowski, Inc.
6350 NE 4th Avenue
P.O. Box 381594
Miami, FL 33138

8. Faith H. Hektoen and Jeanne B. Rinehart, eds., *Toys to Go: A Guide to the Use of Realia in Libraries* (Chicago: American Library Association, 1976), 8.

9. Joanne F. Oppenheim, *Buy Me! Buy Me! The Bank Street Guide to Choosing Toys for Children* (New York: Pantheon, 1987).

Approximate age	What children are like	Types of good toys and worthwhile activities
Birth to 3 months	Begin to smile at people, coo Follow moving person or object with eyes Prefer faces and bright colors Reach, discover hands, kick feet, lift head Suck with pleasure Cry, but often are soothed when held Turn head toward sounds	Rattle, large rings, squeeze or sucking toys Lullabies, nursery rhymes, poems Bright pictures of faces hung so baby can see them Bells firmly attached to baby's wrist, ankle, booties Cardboard or vinyl books with high-contrast illustrations to stand in baby's view Brightly patterned crib sheets Mobile with parts visible from baby's position
4 to 6 months	Prefer parents and older siblings to other people Repeat actions that have interesting results Listen intently, respond when spoken to Laugh, gurgle, imitate sounds Explore hands and feet, put objects in mouth Sit when propped, roll over, scoot, bounce Grasp objects without using thumbs, bat at hanging objects Smile often	Soft doll, texture ball, socks with bright designs Toys that make noise when batted, squeezed, or mouthed Measuring spoons, teething toy Cloth, soft vinyl books with bright pictures to grasp, chew, & shake Pictures of faces covered in plastic, hung at child's level; unbreakable mirror Fingerplays, simple songs, peek-a-boo Socks with bright designs or faces
7 to 12 months	Remember simple events, form simple concepts Identify themselves, body parts, voices of familiar people Understand own name, other common words Say first meaningful words Explore, bang, or shake objects with hands Find hidden objects, put objects in and out of containers Sit alone Creep, pull themselves up to stand, walk May seem shy or become upset with strangers	All of the above *plus* Rag and baby dolls, stuffed animals, puppets Container for large beads, blocks, balls Nesting toy or plastic containers Board books to read, old magazines to tear Recordings of voices, animal sounds, music Wooden blocks, large soft blocks Water toys that float Rubber or large plastic balls Soft plastic or wood vehicle with wheels Games like peek-a-boo

Age	Children	Some good toys
1 to 1½ years	Imitate adult actions Speak and understand more words and ideas Enjoy stories Experiment with objects Walk steadily, climb stairs Assert independence, but strongly prefer familiar people Recognize ownership of objects Develop friendships, but also play alone Are beginning to understand what adults want them to do, but do not yet have the ability to control themselves	All of the above *plus* Surprise or music box Puzzles, 2 to 6 large pieces with knobs Books/recordings with songs, rhymes, simple stories, & pictures Wide watercolor markers, nontoxic fat crayons, large blank paper Geometric, unit, or cardboard blocks People and animals, vehicles: wood or rubber Pounding bench Sand & water play: plastic measuring cups, boats, containers, washable doll Large cardboard box to crawl in Toys that jingle or move when used Kitchen cupboard of *safe* pots, pans, lids, and utensils.
1½ to 2 years	Solve problems Speak and understand even more Show pride in accomplishments, like to help with tasks Exhibit more body control, run Play more with others Begin pretend play	Self-help toys: sorting box, holes with pegs Large spools or beads to string Books with large colorful illustrations, short stories Soft dough clay, bells, drum Small broom, sponge, camera, pots & pans Shopping cart, wagon, steerable riding toy; toy telephone, washable doll
2 to 3½ years	Enjoy learning new skills Learn language rapidly Are always on the go Have some sense of danger Gain more control of hands and fingers Frustrated easily Act more independent, but are still dependent, too Act out familiar scenes	Wood puzzles with 4 to 20 pieces Pegboards, sewing cards, stacking toys, picture lotto, dominoes Picture/story books, poems about familiar things Classical, folk, children's music Finger or tempera paint, ½" brushes, blunt scissors, white glue Unit blocks & accessories, wood train set with large pieces Hammer (13 oz steel shanked), soft wood, roofing nails, nailing block Triangle, wood block; texture- & sound-matching games Wagon or wheelbarrow, large rubber ball, riding toy Washable doll with a few clothes, doll bed Dress-up clothes: hats, shoes, shirts; hand puppet

Figure 3. Some good toys and activities for young children. From *Toys: Tools for Learning.* Washington, DC.: National Association for the Education of Young Children, 1985. NAEYC brochure #571. Reprinted with permission.

Brio Scanditoy Corp.
6555 W. Mill Road
Milwaukee, WI 53218

Fisher-Price
Division of Quaker Oats Co.
636 Girard Avenue
East Aurora, NY 14052

Galt and Company, Inc.
63 N. Plains Highway
Wallingford, CT 06492

Gund, Inc.
1 Runyan Lane
Edison, NJ 08818

Johnson & Johnson Child Development Toys
Grandview Road
Skillman, NJ 08558

Lego Systems, Inc.
555 Taylor Road
Enfield, CT 06082

For information about toy libraries, write to the USA Toy Library Association, 104 Wilmot Road, Suite 201, Deerfield, IL 60015. *Toys for Growing—A Guide to Toys That Develop Skills*, by Mary Sinker, is the association's official toy guide and a valuable resource for locating toy companies.

The Parenting Collection

Parents, especially first-time parents, are seeking solid information on how to raise a child. According to Burton White, director of the Center for Parent Education, the most effective way to get information across to parents is through talk and pictures. Only 10 to 15 percent of the parents who use the center prefer to get information by *reading* materials on early child development. Based on this finding, White recommends that librarians purchase quality videotapes on parenting and make them available for home borrowing or in-house use.

Films and Videos

When selecting films and videos for the parenting collection, ask the following questions:

1. Does the video present reliable information, as reflected in the current research?
2. Is the information clearly and interestingly presented?
3. Is the content relevant to the needs and concerns of parents of young children or parents-to-be?

4. Does the video expand parents' understanding of an aspect of early childhood?
5. Is the photography and audiography clear and of good quality?
6. Is the content culturally and socially unbiased?
7. Does the video avoid presenting only one point of view when there is reasonable evidence for more than one?
8. Is the film of appropriate length? (Generally, films less than thirty-five minutes hold the viewers' attention better than longer films.)

A short list of films and videos recommended for the parenting collection can be found at the end of this chapter.

Books

The 10 to 15 percent of parents who prefer to get their information through reading can never seem to get enough reading matter, says White. Librarians can help by choosing the best books and magazines on childcare, selected on the basis of sound research, authority of the author, organization, clarity, and readability. Since the 1960s, roughly three dozen books on how to raise a child have been published each year. In addition, there has been a proliferation of magazines on childcare. With such a flood of material on the market, librarians must learn to discriminate between books based on reliable research and those based on misinformation. White suggests "a healthy skepticism" as the most responsible, professional stance to take when approaching any new parenting publication. White advises librarians not to be deceived by appearances and to note the credentials of the author. Authors of child-rearing books come from a variety of backgrounds and, as a general rule, those backgrounds determine the value of the advice offered. An M.D. is the most appropriate degree for an author of a book on physical health, and a Ph.D. in child development, psychology, or education is best suited for the author of a book on the development of abilities or personality.

Reliable reviews can be found in professional library and early childhood periodicals, such as *Booklist* and *Young Children*. Longer, more critical reviews can be found in the Center for Parent Education's *Newsletter*.[10] In 1987 the center prepared *Book Reviews and Guide to Reading a Popular Book on Early Development and Parenting* for its professional institutes on educating the infant and toddler. This useful guide is available from the center. (See fig. 4 for a comparison of *First Feelings*, by Stanley and Nancy Greenspan, in the *Guide* and in two professional periodicals.) I chose this book for comparison because its coverage in the popular media will have brought it to the attention of many parents and library users.[11]

10. Burton L. White, *Newsletter*. Subscription available from the Center for Parent Education, 55 Chapel Street, Newton, MA 02160.
11. See, for example, Ann Crittenden, "New Insights into Infancy," *New York Times Magazine* (November 13, 1983): 84–85, 90, 95–96; and John Taylor, "Milestones: Charting the Stages in a Child's Emotional Development," *New York* 20:46 (November 23, 1987): 35–39.

Greenspan, Stanley I., M.D. & Nancy Thorndike Greenspan. First Feelings: milestones in the emotional development of your baby and child.

Viking. 1985. c.216p. photogs. index. ISBN 0-670-80386-3. $17.95.   PSYCH

According to the Greenspans (he, Chief of Clinical Infant Development at NIMH, she, a health economist), six emotional stages or "milestones" emerge in a child's first four years of life. (The American Academy of Pediatrics endorses the milestones as evaluation tools.) Using charts, photos, and an informative narrative aimed at college-educated parents, the authors of this breakthrough work competently describe the growth progression from internal self-regulation through emotional thinking. Helpful chapters also include: potential developmental problems; supportive/corrective techniques; an examination of parental obstacles (fears, conflicts) to healthy child rearing. Despite a few drawbacks (not enough examples; single parents receive little attention) essential for child development collections.—*Janice Arenofsky, formerly with Arizona State Lib., Phoenix*

Library Journal 110:77 April 15, 1985. (130w)

GREENSPAN, STANLEY I., and NANCY THORNDIKE GREENSPAN. First Feelings: Milestones in the Emotional Development of Your Baby and Child. (Illus.) NY: Viking. 1985. xii+247pp. $17.95. 84-40471. ISBN 0-670-80386-3. Index; C.I.P.

GA Ac This parent education book is organized around the emotional milestones in the first four years of a child's life. It describes the emotional aspects of child development accurately and reflects warm attitudes toward the growing child. Unfortunately, its conceptual framework, which follows six stages of development, tends to be abstract; discussion of each stage lacks clarity. Specific notes of advice are unclear—for instance, helping the three- to ten-month old baby to "interact throughout [a] range of emotions." This comment has no specific meaning. Advice offered to parents of the 9- to 18-month-old, the stage when an organized sense of self emerges, includes check list items to chart behavior, such as "recovers from anger in a few minutes" and "able to use objects like comb or telephone in a semi-realistic manner." Such broad and generalized statements do not guide a parent's interpretation of the child's actions very well, and interpretation will vary from parent to parent. This book's approach is simplistic and does not take into account special situations that affect child rearing, especially those concerning race or single parenthood—*Donald Brieland, Univ. of Illinois, Chicago, IL*

Science Books & Films 21:296 May/June 1986. (220w)

Figure 4.   One book, three reviews

In contrast to the two short reviews on the previous page, the Center for Parent Education's review by Burton White runs more than 1,700 words. Following a description of the contents, White refers to the division in the field of child development research between "people who are interested in the so-called 'hard' topics, e.g., the development of physical abilities, perceptual skills, language, intelligence, etc., and those who are interested in the so-called 'soft' topics, e.g., the parent-child relationship, self-concept, creativity, emotional well-being, and other such topics." White says he approaches a book such as *First Feelings*, which falls in the latter category, with the attitude "[I] would rather have somebody investigate subjects that I value highly using the best methods he can than remain safely in the work that can be done with greater validity but does not address what I consider to be the most important issues." Nevertheless, White finds the Greenspans' book full of "adult-amorphism, that is, the projection of some of one's own capacities as an adult into the mind of the baby." Quoting passages from the book, White comments that he knows of no basis for the notions expressed and that, in some instances, "the authors' lengthy experience in situations of emotional distress impinges inappropriately on the topic at hand.... As is so often the case with writings by people with one or another specialty, there is the risk of bringing indications of pathological or mildly pathological behavior into the description of the ordinary course of events."

White notes the scarcity of books that address emotional development seriously and comments that some sections of the book are "first rate." He concludes, "In my opinion, this book makes for a good beginning on a very important subject. I would recommend it for professionals, but frankly not for parents—especially not for first-time parents. Professionals who are knowledgeable about early development can take what is good from this book and will profit by adding that to their own backgrounds. However, I think parents will very probably be misled too often and frightened too often, so that the book may actually hinder rather than help their efforts."

Figure 4. (continued)

A vertical file collection of clippings from newspapers, magazines, pamphlets, and other materials of interest to parents and other child caregivers is a valuable resource (see list of suggested subject headings in fig. 5). Many child-oriented businesses, such as manufacturers of baby products (including Beech-Nut, Gerber, and Johnson & Johnson, to name a few), publish in-house newsletters and magazines that are available free to the public. Quantities of twenty-five, fifty, and one hundred are often free to libraries for distribution at workshops.

Adoption	
Allergies	Imaginary playmates
Babysitting	Infant care
Bilingualism	Infants—premature
Breast feeding	Intellectual development
Child abuse	Language development
Childbirth	Literacy (how children learn to
Childcare agencies (list local, state, and national)	read and write)
Child development	Montessori education
Childhood illnesses	Music, movement, and dance
Children's literature and reading	Nutrition
Child support	Play
Crying—infant	Pregnancy/prenatal care
Day care	Safety
Day care centers (list local)	Self-esteem
Disabled children, special needs of	Sibling rivalry
Discipline	Single parenting
Divorce, effect on children	Sleep
Drug abuse	Speech
Fears	Stepparenting
First aid	Teen parenting
Foster parenting	Television viewing
Gifted children	Temperament
Hearing	Toddlerhood
Hyperactivity	Toilet training
	Toys
	Vision

Figure 5. 50 subject headings suggested for a beginning parenting collection vertical file

Librarians can assist parents by compiling booklists on parenting topics and preparing simple, but attractive, brochures on ways of sharing literature with young children. These booklists and brochures can be distributed at the library, in clinics, in pediatric waiting rooms, and at other places where parents are likely to gather.

A few comments about the location of the parenting collection may be appropriate here. The location of the parenting collection should be determined by such factors as (1) availability of space, (2) patterns of use, and (3) hours when the children's room is open. Even if the parenting collection is located in the adult department, each children's room should have a small collection of parenting books easily visible to parents because their first exposure to the library may be through the children's room. The children's librarian is often the first person the parents meet in the library. Often the parents have not used the library before bringing their children to the parent-child literature-sharing program. For example, after a toddler storytime, one mother asked the librarian how she herself might obtain a library card. Another asked about film programs for young children. Such questions indicate that for many parents the children's room is the door to the whole library.

The following titles are suggested for an initial parenting collection.

Books

Alvino, James, and the editors of *Gifted Children Monthly. A Parent's Guide to Raising a Gifted Child*. Boston: Little, Brown, 1985.

Ames, Louise Bates. *Questions Parents Ask*. New York: Clarkson N. Potter, 1988.

_____, et al. *The Gesell Institute's Child from One to Six*. New York: Harper, 1979.

_____, Frances L. Ilg, and Carol Chase Haber. *Your One-Year-Old*. New York: Dell, 1982. (See also *Your Two-Year-Old* and *Your Three-Year-Old* in this series.)

Baghban, Marcia. *Our Daughter Learns to Read and Write: A Case Study from Birth to Three*. Newark, Del.: International Reading Assoc., 1984.

Baker, Susan, and the staff of Boston Children's Hospital. *Parents' Guide to Nutrition: Healthy Eating from Birth through Adolescence*. Reading, Mass.: Addison-Wesley, 1987.

Baldwin, Rahima. *You Are Your Child's First Teacher*. Berkeley, Calif.: Celestial Arts, 1989.

Balter, Lawrence, with Anita Shreve. *Dr. Balter's Child Sense: Understanding and Handling the Common Problems of Infancy and Early Childhood*. New York: Simon & Schuster, 1985.

_____. *Who's in Control? Dr. Balter's Guide to Discipline without Conflict*. New York: Poseidon Press, 1988.

Bayless, Kathleen M., and Marjorie E. Ramsey. *Music: A Way of Life for the Young Child*. 2nd ed. St. Louis, Mo.: Mosby, 1982.

Beck, Joan. *How to Raise a Brighter Child: The Case for Early Learning*. Rev. ed. New York: Pocket Books, 1975.

Berg, Leila. *Reading and Loving*. New York: Rutledge & Kegan, 1977.

Bissex, Glenda. *GNYS AT WRK: A Child Learns to Write and Read*. Boston: Harvard University Press, 1980.

Bosque, Elena, and Sheila Watson. *Safe and Sound: How to Prevent and Treat the Most Common Childhood Emergencies*. New York: St. Martin's Press, 1989.

Boston Children's Medical Center and Richard I. Feinbloom. *Child Health Encyclopedia*. New York: Delacorte, 1975.

Brazelton, T. Berry. *Infants and Mothers: Differences in Development*. New York: Delacorte, 1983.

_____. *Toddlers and Parents: A Declaration of Independence*. New York: Delacorte, 1974.

Brown, Laurie Krasny. *Toddler Time: A Book to Share with Your Toddler*. Illustrated by Marc Brown. Boston: Little, Brown, 1990. (See also *Baby Time* by the Browns.)

Burck, Frances Wells. *Baby Sense: A Practical and Supportive Guide to Baby Care*. New York: St. Martin's Press, 1979.

Bush, Richard. *A Parent's Guide to Child Therapy*. New York: Delacorte, 1980.

Butler, Dorothy. *Babies Need Books*. 2nd ed. New York: Penguin, 1988.

_____. *Cushla and Her Books*. Boston: Horn Book, 1980.

Callahan, Sidney Cornelia. *Parenting: Principles and Politics of Parenthood*. New York: Penguin, 1974.

Carson, Rachel. *The Sense of Wonder*. New York: Harper, 1956.

Cascardi, Andrea E. *Good Books to Grow On: A Guide to Building Your Child's Library from Birth to Age Five*. New York: Warner, 1985.

Chess, Stella, and Alexander Thomas. *Know Your Child: An Authoritative Guide for Today's Parents*. New York: Basic Books, 1987.

Children's Television Workshop Family Living Series. *Parents' Guide to Feeding Your Kids Right*. New York: Prentice-Hall, 1989.

_____. *Parents' Guide to Raising Kids Who Love to Learn*. New York: Prentice-Hall, 1989.

Copperman, Paul. *Taking Books to Heart: How to Develop a Love of Reading in Your Child*. Reading, Mass.: Addison-Wesley, 1986.

Crago, Maureen, and Hugh Crago. *Prelude to Literacy: A Preschool Child's Encounter with Picture and Story*. Carbondale: Southern Illinois University Press, 1983.

Cuthbertson, Joanne, and Susie Schevill. *Helping Your Child Sleep through the Night*. Garden City, N.Y.: Doubleday, 1985.

De Villiers, Peter A. and Jill G. De Villiers. *Early Language*. Cambridge, Mass.: Harvard University Press, 1979.

Dodson, Fitzhugh. *How to Single Parent*. New York: Harper, 1987.

Dombro, Amy Laura, and Leah Wallach. *The Ordinary Is Extraordinary: How Children under Three Learn*. New York: Simon & Schuster, 1988.

Dreskin, Wendy, and William Dreskin. *The Day Care Decision: What's Best for You and Your Child*. New York: M. Evans, 1983.

Dzama, Mary Ann. *Getting Your Child Ready to Read*. New York: John Wiley, 1983.

Elkind, David. *Miseducation: Preschoolers at Risk*. New York: Knopf, 1987.

Fisher, John J. *Toys to Grow With! Infants and Toddlers*. New York: Putnam, 1986.

Fraiberg, Selma. *The Magic Years: Understanding and Handling the Problems of Early Childhood*. New York: Scribner, 1959, 1984.

Friedland, Ronnie, and Carol Kort, eds. *The Mothers' Book: Shared Experiences*. Boston: Houghton Mifflin, 1981.

Galinsky, Ellen, and Judy David. *The Preschool Years*. New York: New York Times Books, 1988.

Gillis, Jack, and Mary Ellen Fise. *The Children's Catalog: A Consumer Guide to Buying the Safest and Best Products for Your Children, Newborns through Age Five*. New York: Pocket Books, 1986.

Greene, Diana S. *79 Ways to Calm a Crying Baby*. New York: Pocket Books, 1988.

Hamberger, Lars. *A Child Is Born*. Photographed by Lennart Nilsson. New ed. New York: Delacorte, 1990.

Harding, Edith, and Philip Riley. *The Bilingual Family: A Handbook for Parents*. New York: Cambridge University Press, 1986.

Heckinger, Grace. *How to Raise a Street-Smart Child*. New York: Ballantine, 1984.

Jalongo, Mary Renck. *Young Children and Picture Books*. Washington, D.C.: National Association for the Education of Young Children, 1988.

Johnson & Johnson Child Development Publications. *The First Wondrous Year* and *Your Baby*. Edited by Richard A. Chase, M.D., and Richard R. Rubin, Ph.D. New York: Collier Books, 1979, 1984.

Jones, Sandy, and Werner Freitag and the editors of Consumer Reports Books. *A Guide to Baby Products*. Mt. Vernon, N.Y.: Consumers Union, 1988.

Kaban, Barbara. *Choosing Toys for Children from Birth to Five*. New York: Schocken, 1979.

Katzev, Aphra R., and Nancy H. Bragdon. *Child Care Solution: A Parents' Guide to Finding Child Care You Can Trust*. New York: Avon, 1990.

Lamme, Linda Leonard. *Growing Up Reading: Sharing with Your Children the Joys of Reading*. Washington, D.C.: Acropolis Books, Ltd., 1985.

————, et al. *Raising Readers: A Guide to Sharing Literature with Young Children*. New York: Walker, 1980.

Lansky, Bruce. *Baby Talk*. Deephaven, Minn.: Meadowbrook Press, 1986.

Lansky, Vicki. *Getting Your Baby to Sleep (and Back to Sleep)* and *Toilet Training*. Practical Parenting Series. New York: Bantam, 1985, 1984.

Lapinski, Susan, and Michael Decourcy Hinds. *In a Family Way*. Boston: Little, Brown, 1982.

Larrick, Nancy. *A Parent's Guide to Children's Reading*. 5th ed. New York: Doubleday, 1982.

Leach, Penelope. *The First Six Months: Getting Together with Your Baby.* New York: Knopf, 1987.

———. *Your Baby and Child: From Birth to Age Five.* Rev. ed. New York: Knopf, 1989.

Lehane, Stephen. *Help Your Baby Learn: 100 Piaget-based Activities for the First Two Years of Life.* New York: Prentice-Hall, 1976.

Leight, Lynn. *Raising Sexually Healthy Children: A Loving Guide for Parents, Teachers and Care-givers.* New York: Avon, 1990.

Lindsay, Jeanne Warren. *Teens Parenting: The Challenge of Babies and Toddlers.* Buena Park, Calif.: Morning Glory Press, 1981.

Loman, Kay. *Of Cradles and Careers: A Guide to Reshaping Your Job to Include a Child in Your Life.* Franklin Park, Ill.: La Leche League, 1984.

Lynch-Fraser, Diane. *Danceplay: Creative Movement for Very Young Children.* New York: Walker, 1982.

McCoy, Kathleen. *Solo Parenting: Your Essential Guide: How to Find the Balance between Parenthood and Personhood.* New York: NAL Books/New American Library, 1987.

McMullen, Kate Hall. *How to Choose Good Books for Kids.* Reading, Mass.: Addison-Wesley, 1984.

Mahoney, Ellen, and Leah Wilcox. *Ready, Set, Read: Best Books to Prepare Preschoolers.* Metuchen, N.J.: Scarecrow Press, 1985.

Marzollo, Jean. *Supertot.* New York: Harper, 1977.

Mayer, Rochelle. *Beginning Together.* New York: St. Martin's Press, 1983.

Maynard, Fredelle. *The Child Care Crisis.* New York: Viking, 1985.

Miller, Karen. *Things to Do with Toddlers and Twos.* Marshfield, Mass.: Telshare, 1984.

Morris, Monica. *Last-chance Children: Growing Up with Older Parents.* New York: Columbia University Press, 1988.

Nelson, Christine A., M.D., and Susan Pescar. *Should I Call the Doctor?* New York: Warner Books, 1986.

Nolte, Judy, ed. *The First Year of Life.* New York: American Baby Magazine, 1981.

Oppenheim, Joanne F. *Buy Me! Buy Me! The Bank Street Guide to Choosing Toys for Children.* New York: Pantheon, 1987. (See also Oppenheim et al., *Choosing Books for Kids: Choosing the Right Book for the Right Child at the Right Time.* A Bank Street Book. [Ballatine, 1986].)

Pagnoni, Mario. *Computers and Small Fries: A Computer-Readiness Guide for Parents of Tots, Toddlers, and Other Minors.* Wayne, N.J.: Avery, 1986.

Pogrebin, Letty Cottin. *Growing Up Free: Raising Your Child in the 80s.* New York: Bantam, 1980.

Pruett, Kyle D. *The Nurturing Father.* New York: Warner Books, 1987.

Pulaski, Mary Ann. *Your Baby's Mind and How It Grows: Piaget's Theory for Parents.* New York: Harper, 1978.

RIF Guide for Encouraging Young Readers. Washington, D.C.: Reading Is Fundamental, 1987.

Rocissano, Lorraine, and Jean Grasso Fitzpatrick. *Helping Baby Talk: A Pressure-free Approach to Your Child's First Words from Birth to 3 Years.* New York: Avon Skylight Press, 1990.

Roemer, Joan, as told to Barbara Austin. *Two to Four from 9 to 5: The Adventures of a Daycare Provider.* New York: Harper, 1989.

Rudman, Marsha Kabakow, Anne Marjus Pierce, and the editors of Consumer Reports Books. *For Love of Reading: A Parent's Guide to Encouraging Young Readers from Infancy through Age 5.* Mount Vernon, N.Y.: Consumers Union, 1988.

Satter, Ellyn. *How to Get Your Kid to Eat...But Not Too Much.* Palo Alto, Calif.: Bull Publishing, 1987.

Segal, Marilyn. *In Time and with Love.* New York: Newmarket Press, 1988. (About premature infants.)

_____ , and Don Adcock. *Your Child at Play: Two to Three Years.* New York: Newmarket Press, 1985. (Other titles in this three-volume series include *Your Child at Play: Birth to One Year* and *Your Child at Play: One to Two Years.*)

Shiff, Eileen, ed. *Experts Advise Parents: A Guide to Raising Loving, Responsible Children.* New York: Delacorte, 1987.

Singer, Dorothy, and Jerome Singer. *Partners in Play.* New York: Harper, 1977.

Spock, Benjamin. *Dr. Spock on Parenting: Sensible Advice for Today.* New York: Simon & Schuster, 1988.

_____, and Michael B. Rothenberg. *Baby and Child Care.* Rev. ed. New York: Dutton, 1985.

Stallibrass, Allison. *The Self-Respecting Child: Development through Spontaneous Play.* Reading, Mass.: Addison-Wesley, 1989.

Stewart, Arlene. *Childproofing Your Home.* Reading, Mass.: Addison-Wesley, 1984.

Sutton-Smith, Brian. *How to Play with Your Children.* New York: Hawthorne Press, 1974.

Sweet, O. Robin, and Mary-Ellen Siegel. *The Nanny Connection.* New York: Atheneum, 1987.

Szasz, Suzanne. *The Unspoken Language of Children.* New York: W. W. Norton, 1980.

Talcacs, Carol Addison. *Enjoy Your Gifted Child.* Syracuse, N.Y.: Syracuse University Press, 1986.

Taylor, Denny, and Dorothy S. Strickland. *Family Storybook Reading.* Portsmouth, N.H.: Heinemann, 1986.

Trelease, Jim. *The New Read-Aloud Handbook.* 2nd rev. ed. New York: Penguin, 1989.

Ulene, Art, and Steven Shelov. *Bringing Out the Best in Your Baby.* New York: Macmillan, 1986.

White, Burton L. *The First Three Years of Life.* Rev. ed. New York: Prentice-Hall, 1985.

Winkel, Lois, and Sue Kimmel. *Mother Goose Comes First: An Annotated Guide to the Best Books and Recordings for Your Preschool Child.* New York: Holt, 1990.

Magazines and Newsletters

American Baby Magazine
P.O. Box 51188
Boulder, CO 80321-1188

Baby Talk
Parenting Unlimited, Inc.
636 Avenue of the Americas
New York, NY 10011

Doubletalk (for parents of twins, triplets, quads, quints)
P.O. Box 412
Amelia, OH 45102

Exceptional Parent
P.O. Box 3000, Dept. EP
Denville, NJ 07834-9919

Extensions (High/Scope curriculum newsletter)
High/Scope Press
600 N. River Street
Ypsilanti, MI 48198

First-Time Parents
Cahners Publishing Co.
475 Park Avenue South
New York, NY 10016

Growing Child and *Growing Parent*
Dunn and Hargitt, Inc.
22 N. Second Street
Lafayette, IN 47902

Mothering (winner of the 1990 Utne Reader Alternate Press Award)
Peggy O'Mara
P.O. Box 1690
Santa Fe, NM 87504

Parent and preschooler Newsletter
P.O. Box 1851
Garden City, NY 11530

Parents' Choice
P.O. Box 185
Waban, MA 02168

Parents Magazine
P.O. Box 3055
Harlan, IA 51593-2199

Pediatrics for Parents (newsletter)
P.O. Box 1069
Bangor, ME 04401

Pre-K Today (Scholastic)
P.O. Box 3022
Southeastern, PA 19398-3022

The Pre-Parent Advisor, The New Parent Advisor, The Parent Advisor
(sponsored by Johnson & Johnson)
13–30 Corp.
505 Market Street
Knoxville, TN 37902

Single Parent
(a publication of Parents Without Partners, Inc.)
7910 Woodmont Avenue
Suite 1000
Bethesda, MD 20814

Working Mother
230 Park Avenue
New York, NY 10169

Young Children
National Association for the
    Education of Young Children
1834 Connecticut Avenue, NW
Washington, DC 20009-5786

Films and Videos

Babies Are People Too. Churchill Films, 1986. 27 min. Video.

Baby Comes Home. Karl-Lorimar Home Video, 1985. 50 min. Video.

Care of the Infant: Animal and Human. Perennial Education, Inc., 1977. 22 min. 16mm film.

Choosing the Best in Children's Video. (Features Christopher Reeve as host.) ALA Graphics, American Library Association, 1990. 35 min. Video.

Choosing the Right Toys for Babies and Toddlers. (Features Michael K. Meyerhoff of the Center for Parent Education.) Foxhall Video, Inc., 1985. 30 min. Video.

Drop Everything and Read. (Features Fred Rogers, Jim Trelease, and others.) Films for the Humanities and Sciences, 1986. 28 min. 16mm film and video.

Early Childhood Safety. Milner-Fenwick, 1986. 16 min. 16mm film and video.

Everybody Rides the Carousel—Part I: A Joyous Journey into the Child's World and an Overview of the Early Years of Life. (Presents Erikson's theory of ego crises.) Pyramid Films, 1975. 24 min. 16mm film.

Everyday Miracle: Birth. Films, Inc., 1981. 30 min. Video.

First Days of Parenthood. Milner-Fenwick, 1986. 15 min. 16mm film and video.

The First Three Years. (Eight 25-min. programs and a 55-min. summary program featuring Burton L. White.) Center for Parent Education, n.d. 16mm film and video.

The Foundations of Reading and Writing. Queens College of the City University of New York/Campus Film Distributors, 1975. 40 min. 16mm film.

Growing into Parenthood. Vida Health Communications, 1986. 29 min. 16mm film and video.

Help! I'm a New Parent. Churchill Films, 1979. 24 min. 16mm film.

Mastering the Tasks of Toddlerhood. Davidson Films, 1990. 25 min. 16mm film and video.

New Relations. Plainsong Productions, 1980. 34 min. 16mm film.

Oh Brother, My Brother. Pyramid Films, 1979. 14 min. 16mm film.

Prenatal Care. Milner-Fenwick, 1977. 11 min. 16mm film and video.

Read to Me: Libraries, Books, and Your Baby. Greater Vancouver Library Federation, 1987. 15 min. Video.

The Terrific Twos. (Features T. Berry Brazelton.) Professional Research, 1986. 15 min. Video.

What Every Baby Knows. (T. Berry Brazelton hosts four programs: "Most Common Questions about Newborns, Infants and Toddlers"; "The Working Parents"; "A Guide to Pregnancy and Childbirth"; and "On Being a Father.") Family Home Entertainment/available from Upbeat Videos, 1984 and 1985. 60 to 70 min. Video.

What's So Great about Books. Orlando Public Library, 1977. 15 min. 16mm film.

The World of Three. National Film Board of Canada, 1966. 28 min. 16mm film.

Your Child: 6 Months–12 Months. Milner-Fenwick, 1985. 10:55 min. 16mm film and video.

Your Child: 18 Months–24 Months. Milner-Fenwick, 1985. 10:58 min. 16 mm film and video.

Appendix
Directory of Producers and Distributors
Recordings

A & M Records, Inc.
1416 N. La Brea Avenue
Hollywood, CA 90028

Alcazar Records; see Silo.

American Melody Records
P.O. Box 270
Guilford, CT 06437

B/B Records
570 N. Arden Boulevard
Los Angeles, CA 90004

Caedmon Records
1995 Broadway
New York, NY 10023

CMS Records, Inc.
226 Washington Street
Mt. Vernon, NY 10553

Columbia/CBS Records, Inc.
51 W. 52nd Street
New York, NY 10019

Earth Mother Productions, Inc.
P.O. Box 43204
Tucson, AZ 85753

Educational Activities, Inc.
P.O. Box 392
Freeport, NY 11520

Elephant Records/distributed by Silo, Inc.; see Silo.

A Gentle Wind
P.O. Box 3103
Albany, NY 12203

Golden Glow Recordings/ distributed by Silo, Inc.; see Silo.

J. Aaron Brown & Associates, Inc.
1508 16th Avenue South
Nashville, TN 37212

Jazz Cat Productions
345 S. McDowell Boulevard
Suite 203
Petaluma, CA 94954

Kids Records
P.O. Box 670 Station A
Toronto, Ontario M5W 1G2
   Canada

Kimbo Educational Records
10–16 N. 3rd Avenue
P.O. Box 477
Long Branch, NJ 07740

Lightyear Entertainment/Records
350 5th Avenue, Suite 5108
New York, NY 10118

London Records Ltd.
c/o Polygram Records
825 8th Avenue
New York, NY 10019

Marlboro Records, Inc.
845 Marlboro Spring Road
Kennett Square, PA 19348

MCA Distributing Corporation
70 Universal City Plaza
Universal City, CA 91608

RCA Records
1133 Avenue of the Americas
New York, NY 10036

Red Rover Records
P.O. Box 124
Lake Bluff, IL 60044

Rounder Records
1 Camp Street
Cambridge, MA 02140

Silo, Inc./Alcazar Records
P.O. Box 429
Waterbury, VT 05676

Smithsonian/Folkways
Birch Tree Group, Ltd.
180 Alexander Street
Princeton, NJ 08540

Films/Videos

A & M Video
1416 N. La Brea Avenue
Hollywood, CA 90028

ALA Graphics
American Library Association
50 E. Huron Street
Chicago, IL 60611

American School Publishers
Box 408
Hightstown, NJ 08520

Campus Film Distributors Corp.
24 Depot Square
Tuckahoe, NY 10707

Center for Parent Education
55 Chapel Street
Newton, MA 02160

Churchill Films
12210 Nebraska Avenue
Los Angeles, CA 90025

Davidson Films
231 E Street
Davis, CA 05616

Direct Cinema, Ltd.
Box 69799
Los Angeles, CA 90069

Films for the Humanities and
  Sciences
P.O. Box 2053
Princeton, NJ 08543

Films, Inc.
5547 N. Ravenswood Avenue
Chicago, IL 60640

Foxhall Video, Inc.
5108 Palisade Lane, NW
Washington, DC 20016

Greater Vancouver Library
  Federation
110-6545 Bonsor Avenue
Burnaby, BC V5H 1H3, Canada

International Film Bureau
332 S. Michigan Avenue
Chicago, IL 60604

Karl-Lorimar Home Video
17942 Cowan Avenue
Irvine, CA 92714

Live Oak Media
Box 34
Ancramdale, NY 12503

Milner-Fenwick
2125 Greenspring Drive
Timonium, MD 21093

National Film Board of Canada
1251 Avenue of the Americas
New York, NY 10020

Orlando Public Library
10 N. Rosalind Street
Orlando, FL 32801

Perennial Education Inc.
930 Pitner Avenue
Evanston, IL 60202

Phoenix/BFA Films and Video
468 Park Avenue S.
New York, NY 10016

Plainsong Productions
47 Halifax Street
Jamaica Plain, MA 02130

Professional Research
930 Pitner Avenue
Evanston, IL 60202

Pyramid Films
Box 1048
Santa Monica, CA 90406

Random House, Inc.
201 E. 50th Street
New York, NY 10022

UPBEAT
163 Joralemon Street, Suite 1250
Brooklyn, NY 11201

Vida Health Communications
335 Huron Avenue
Cambridge, MA 02138

Weston Woods Studios
Weston, CT 06883

Computer Programs

American School Publishers
P.O. Box 408
Hightstown, NJ 08520

Davidson & Associates, Inc.
3135 Kashiwa Street
Torrance, CA 90505

DLM Teaching Resources
1 DLM Park
Allen, TX 75002

Learning Company
6493 Kaiser Drive
Fremont, CA 94555

Spinnaker Software Corporation
1 Kendall Square
Cambridge, MA 02139

Springboard Software
7808 Creekridge Circle
Minneapolis, MN 55435

Sunburst Communications, Inc.
39 Washington Avenue
Pleasantville, NY 10570

Weekly Reader Software from
    Optimum Resources, Inc.
10 Station Place
Norfolk, CT 06058

Toy Manufacturers and Suppliers

For mail-order catalogs, write to:

ABC School Supply, Inc.
3312 N. Berkeley Lake Road
P.O. Box 100019
Duluth, GA 30136-9419

Childcraft Center
150 E. 58th Street
New York, NY 10022

Childcraft, Inc.
20 Kilmer Road
P.O. Box 3143
Edison, NJ 08818-3143

Constructive Playthings
1227 E. 119th Street
Grandview, MO 64030

Creative Playthings, Inc.
Edinburg Road
Cranbury, NJ 98512

Heads Up/Early Learning
    Institute
445 E. Charleston Road
Suite 9
Palo Alto, CA 94306

Johnson & Johnson Child
    Development Toys
Stratmer Station
P.O. Box 7407
Bridgeport, CT 06650

Learning Materials Workshop
58 Henry Street
Burlington, VT 05401

Lego Systems, Inc.
P.O. Box 640
Enfield, CT 06082

Nienhuis Montessori
    International B.V.
P.O. Box 16
7020 AA
Zelhem (Gld.), Holland

Toys to Grow On
P.O. Box 17
Long Beach, CA 90801

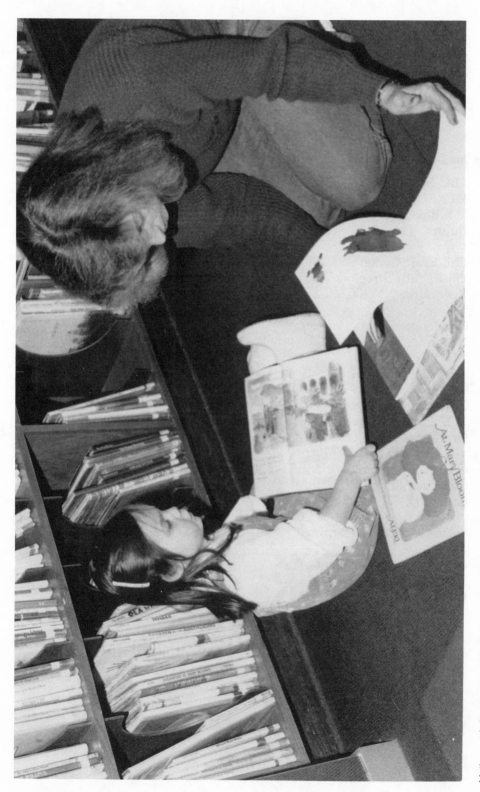

Mother and daughter ponder their selections at the Saratoga Springs (N.Y.) Public Library. Photo credit: Ellen deLalla.

chapter

5

PROGRAM PLANNING

Parenting Programs

The primary purpose of library service to early childhood is to introduce parents to the library as a parenting information center and to demonstrate ways of sharing books and nonbook materials with very young children. As the librarian, keep in mind that whenever you affect a parent, you affect the life of a child.

Babies are not passive creatures, as was once supposed. Most babies are born with all five senses intact, and all actively seek stimulus of the senses. This innate curiosity is the basis of learning. Parents can either encourage or put a damper on the child's impulse toward learning. Through his work in the Harvard Preschool Project, Burton White discovered that first-time parents spend twice as much time with their child as parents of two or more children. White advises librarians to focus on first-time parents and on people who have just learned that they are going to have their first child. Not only are childcare topics of interest to such people, but programs at the library offer first-time parents an opportunity to interact with, and to gain reassurance from, other new parents. As a starter, White suggests a panel discussion on a particular aspect of child development—for example, how children learn to read, from the viewpoint of different disciplines. *The Foundations of Reading and Writing* film (see Films and Videos on pages 65–66) might precede the discussion. This film demonstrates the connections between hearing stories read aloud and later interest in books and reading. Parents learn that putting a simple puzzle together helps a child distinguish shapes and discover that parts can be put together to make a whole. Later the child will put letters together to form words and words to form sentences.

Other suggestions from White include offering parents and children literature-sharing programs that introduce first-time parents to the library and its resources, to developmentally appropriate books and activities, and to ways of sharing books with their children[1]; making an in-house video on

1. See, for example, Floyd C. Dickson and Janice D. Smuda, Preschool Services and Parent Education Committee, Association for Library Service to Children, *How to Raise a Reader: Sharing Books with Infants and Toddlers* (Chicago: American Library Association, 1990).

Putting together a simple puzzle helps a child distinguish shapes and discover that parts can be put together to make a whole. Children's Center, Gail Borden Public Library, Elgin, Illinois. Photo credit: Cliff E. Lohs.

how to read a story aloud; and scheduling "open house" one morning a week when parents can interact with other parents and their children in the early childhood area of the library.

Bedtime is a favorite read-aloud time. White would like librarians to encourage parents to read aloud at other times, such as on visits to the pediatrician, during feeding times, or just before naptime. Another idea is for parents to keep a diary of their child's responses to stories. Librarians can stimulate this type of activity by asking "What kinds of stories does your child enjoy most?", "Have you noticed any changes in the way your child responds to stories over a period of time?", and similar questions. Shelving books like *Our Daughter Learns to Read and Write: A Case Study from Birth to Three*, by Marcia Baghban, Glenda Bissex' *GNYS AT WRK*, Dorothy Butler's *Cushla and Her Books*, and *Prelude to Literacy: A Preschool Child's Encounter with Picture and Story*, by Maureen and Hugh Crago will also encourage this type of activity.[2]

First Steps to Literacy: Library Programs for Parents, Teachers, and Caregivers, prepared by the Preschool Services and Parent Education Committee of the Association for Library Service to Children and published by ALA in 1990, is full of excellent advice on programming, planning, and presentation and includes a complete guide to seven library programs, from "First Books for Your Baby" to "Finding Books for Special Needs." Each program guide gives the intended audience, the suggested length of time for the program, the program's goals and objectives, and hints for planning and presentation. Books and other resources for use in the program are listed. Figure 6 shows a sample.

Parent and Child Literature-sharing Programs

Storytimes for children under age three are informational programs designed to introduce parents and caregivers to library materials and services and to demonstrate effective ways of sharing literature with very young children. The goals of the parent-child literature-sharing program are:

1. To bring parents an awareness of quality books and nonprint materials developmentally appropriate for young children
2. To give parents participatory experiences in sharing literature with their children and an opportunity to observe effective storytelling
3. To introduce the public library as a resource center for parents
4. To provide a place for first-time parents to meet
5. To give infants and toddlers a joyous experience so that they will associate books and libraries with pleasure.

2. Marcia Baghban, *Our Daughter Learns to Read and Write: A Case Study from Birth to Three* (Newark, Del.: International Reading Association, 1984); Glenda Bissex, *GNYS AT WRK: A Child Learns to Write and Read* (Boston: Harvard University Press, 1980); Dorothy Butler, *Cushla and Her Books* (Boston: Horn Book, 1980); Maureen Crago and Hugh Crago, *Prelude to Literacy: A Preschool Child's Encounter with Picture and Story*. Carbondale: Southern Illinois University Press, 1983).

1. First Books for Your Baby

CAROLINE FELLER BAUER

INTENDED AUDIENCE: Expectant parents

LENGTH: Forty minutes, plus time to examine books

SUMMARY OF PROGRAM: This lecture and demonstration introduce new and expectant parents to the joys and delights of children's literature. The objective is simply to get the audience excited about children's books. The lecture does not attempt to give reasons why one should read to children; it does attempt to overwhelm the audience with the wonder of children's books.

HINTS FOR PLANNING AND PRESENTATION: This is your big chance to introduce adults to a new, lasting, and useful hobby. The program is not just for first-time parents; invite everyone! But aim your publicity at expectant parents. Take advantage of their enthusiasm and get them interested in books before they are immersed in all the work of parenting. If you can do this, they will continue to explore books for the fun of it as well as for the edification of their children. Be sure to invite dads as well as moms, and include the men in your talk. Keep the group small enough so that everyone can see the pictures in the books you show.

Present your talk in an informal, relaxed manner so your audience will not be afraid to make comments or ask questions.

Exhibit a variety of the newest picture books to show that there is a book for every taste, no matter how conservative or bizarre! Distribute an annotated bibliography to match your book display. I like to develop a new list every year to showcase my favorite new titles.

I. INTRODUCTION

    A. Stress the excitement and pleasure in store for your audience as they begin to learn about the wonderful world of children's books.

    B. Briefly discuss the tremendous increase in the publication of children's books, especially books for babies and toddlers in the past several years.

    C. Point out that bookstores simply do not have the space to display all the books published for young children; supermarkets and toy stores have an even smaller selection. The public library

Figure 6. Sample program in *First Steps to Literacy: Library Programs for Parents, Teachers, and Caregivers* (ALA, 1990), pp. 29-31.

offers the best access to a wide variety of children's books. Encourage your audience to think of children's librarians as subject specialists who can offer them valuable guidance.

II. A LOOK AT THE VARIETY OF "BABY BOOKS" AVAILABLE TODAY

A. Show *Pat the Bunny*.[1] One of the most satisfying baby books was published many years ago. Now considered a classic, Dorothy Kunhardt's *Pat the Bunny* introduces baby to the simple pleasures of playing peek-a-boo, waving good-bye, feeling Daddy's scratchy beard, and patting a soft bunny.

B. Show a selection of *object identification* books. A major parent obsession is teaching a child to communicate. When we visit a foreign country we're always a bit peeved that small children are speaking Chinese or French fluently when we can't even say "thank you." The truth is that it took those children two or three years to learn their native language. It will take your child that long to speak English. You can help by speaking to your child as much as possible and by using the *look say* method with books. There are many children's books that show an object common to the child's world and give the word for that object next to it or underneath it. You'll find words like house, dog, chair. If you live in a climate like Hawaii's, you'll probably be surprised to find the word mittens, but keep in mind that mittens is a word, too.

C. Show examples of cloth and board books. When babies are brand new, they will not be able to hold a book or turn the pages. You, your spouse, Grandma, or Uncle Harry will do that. But as soon as children can reach out they'll grab for the book. This is the time to try board books or cloth books. These books are made for tough handling, grabbing, and biting. A child needs to learn how to grasp a page and turn it, but you cannot expect this to happen for many months.

D. Show sets of books by major authors and illustrators, such as Jan Ormerod, Anne Rockwell, Rosemary Wells, and Peter Spier. These are books written and offered individually but also as part of a group. You'll soon learn the authors' and illustrators' names, and you'll enjoy the books they've produced for older children as your child grows.

1. Dorothy Kunhardt, *Pat the Bunny* (Racine, Wis.: Western Publishing Co., 1942).

Figure 6. (continued)

III. ALTERNATIVE INTRODUCTIONS TO THE WORLD
OF PAPER AND PRINT

    A. Show a variety of magazines with big pictures. Include nature magazines, food magazines, and special magazines like *Life*. Show several full-color mail order catalogs and some illustrated greeting cards. You don't always need a bound book to introduce children to paper and print. These non-book materials can introduce your baby to the world of paper and print as well as any book. You don't need an author's text to go with the pictures. Simply talk to your baby about what is in the pictures.

    B. Show a roll of wax paper; unroll it. One of my favorite gifts for a six-month-old is a roll of waxed paper. The child can learn about paper—by crinkling, pulling, or smashing it—without destroying a book.

IV. READING ALOUD

    A. Encourage parents to read to their children as often as possible—even several times a day. Establish a tradition of the "lunch book" or the "nap book" as well as the "bedtime" book.

    B. Suggest that parents involve the whole family—mom, dad, siblings, and even the family dog—in share-a-book time.

    C. Emphasize that parents should not feel that they have to share a different book every time they read to their children. Young children adore repetition.

V. WHERE TO GO FROM HERE

    A. Distribute an annotated bibliography designed to show the vast range of picture books. Explain that this is a small sampling of the many delightful books published for young children. Over 4,000 children's books are published each year.

    B. Booktalk a few of your favorite new picture books for older children, emphasizing the fantastic variety of books to choose from as children grow and become avid listeners.

    C. Once again, encourage your audience to look for these and other titles at the public library. Leave them with the thought that there is a book for every child and for every adult who wants to share.

Figure 6. (continued)

Before starting a parent-child literature-sharing program, decide on the need. Have parents requested it? Are there many young children in the neighborhood, with few or no similar programs available to them?

Next, consider some practical issues. Is there a place for the group to meet? Are there enough books and other materials to support the program? Is there enough staff? Conscientious children's librarians may burn themselves out trying to keep up with the demand for toddler storytimes by older, better educated parents who want the best for their first-born. In many communities, it is impossible to schedule the number of storytimes demanded by parents. In this case, hard decisions must be made and alternatives considered—short series, one-time series attendance only, training day-care staff and others to conduct storytimes for toddlers, and so on. But there are other communities where teen-age parents, some still children themselves, are unaware of library services that could help them, and communities where people, newly arrived from countries in which library service is not well developed, are totally unaware of what the library has to offer. A balance must be struck between these groups—the one so vocal, the other two often invisible and silent.

At the NYPL/NYU Conference, speaker Ann Carlson emphasized the desirability of librarians placing their efforts on training caregivers in storytelling techniques and in materials selection rather than trying to increase the number of library toddler programs to meet the insatiable demand. Children's librarians differ in philosophy about this, but changing demographics may support an outreach approach. At present, 57 percent of women with children under the age of six work outside the home, as compared with 12 percent in 1950. More than half of all new mothers return to work before their children's first birthdays. By 1995, two-thirds of all preschool children will have mothers in the workforce. However, even those practitioners who agree with Carlson will want to present some programs in the library as a way of keeping in touch with children's responses to new materials and of establishing the library as a place where books and reading are valued. Incidentally, a fifteen-minute toddler program may require two hours' preparation time. One way to make the program more cost effective is to repeat it in local day-care centers.

If, after considering all of the issues presented above, you want to proceed with a program, your next step is to decide on the ages of the participants. Most libraries offer programs for children from eighteen months to three years or for two- to three-year-olds. A few have programs for infants as young as six months. The younger the children, the more the program is targeted toward the parents and caregivers.

Decide on a time for the program. Morning or early evening seems to be the most convenient time for caregivers to participate in a parent-child program. Afternoons often do not work because many toddlers take a nap at that time.

Next, decide how long you will offer the program. Many librarians recommend that the program be limited to once a week over a period of four to six weeks. After a break of a month or so, a new series begins. The new series is usually limited to parents and children who did not attend the first series, as its purpose is to introduce as many parents as possible to ways of sharing literature with their children. However, the length of each series and whether or not the same parents and children can attend should be decided on the basis of a community's needs and a library's resources.

The best publicity for promoting a program is word of mouth, a sign in the library, and flyers distributed in the community. A sample flyer appears as figure 7.

The Children's Services Department
of the
Middle Country Public Library
presents

A
Mother Goose
Nursery Rhyme Program

For: Parents and Children
(Birth - 36 months)
Date: Friday, April 14, 1989
Place: Middle Country Public Library
Main Library, Centereach
Time: 10:00 am
or
10:45 am

In person pre-registration required
District residents only

Figure 7. Sample promotion flyer

Preregistration is a must in order to keep the group small. Ten to twelve infants or toddlers, each accompanied by a parent or caregiver, is a workable-size group. At the time of preregistration inform the parents or caregivers that they must remain with their children throughout the program and give them a copy of "Storytime Do's and Don'ts" (see fig. 8) or something similar.

You may wish to send a follow-up letter to the parent or caregiver a week or so before the program actually begins (see sample letter in fig. 9). Encourage parents to arrive about ten minutes before the program is scheduled to start. Latecomers disrupt the flow of the program, but children who arrive too early may become overly excited or shy while waiting.

Hold the program in a quiet, self-contained area, away from distractions. Ideally, this area should be carpeted. Carpet squares may be used, but they are a safety hazard for crawlers and children just learning to walk.

Young children enjoy ritual. Following the same routine each week gives both children and adults a sense of security. (See Storytime for infants

---

Storytime Do's and Don'ts

The goal of the storytime program is to provide you and your child with an enjoyable library experience based on books and language. The following rules will help us reach that goal.

1. Arrive ten to fifteen minutes before the storytime is scheduled to begin so that your child can receive a name tag and meet the other participants.

2. Wear comfortable clothing so that you can sit on the floor with your child.

3. The program has been designed to include a variety of stories, songs, rhymes, and activities appropriate for toddlers. Some children may participate, while others may be content to just observe. *All adults, however, are expected to participate.*

4. For some children, this will be their first group experience in the library. If your child is restless, leave the room as quietly as possible. This will minimize the distraction for everyone.

If you have any questions, please call me at (telephone number). Thank you for your understanding and cooperation.

Children's Librarian

Figure 8. Sample instructions for parents or caregivers

Storytimes for 2-Year-Olds

(name) _____ is scheduled for storytime on

(day) _____ at (time) _____ am/pm for 20-30 minutes.

It begins on (date) _____ .

For many children this will be their first group experience. To make it a happy one, we ask your cooperation and assistance in the following ways:

1. Please discuss storytime with your child before you come, explaining that there will be stories, fingerplays, puppets, games and songs, and that you will participate together. Young children need to know what is expected of them.
2. Bring only the toddler who is registered. Older or younger children should not be a part of this activity.
3. Attendance is important. Activities of one week are dependent on those shared the week before. Please call if you cannot attend.
4. Once the storytime program is in progress, no one will be admitted to the storyspace. Two-year-olds are easily distracted and latecomers become the focus of attention. Please plan to arrive early.
5. There will be name tags for your child and for yourself. They will help everyone become acquainted and feel at ease.
6. We will hold each program in the StoryRoom and will enter together when it is time to begin. There will be carpet samples on the floor for seating.* Please choose a place to sit with your child on your lap or in front of you.
7. If your child becomes very restless or uncooperative, please step outside for a few seconds. This helps everyone to concentrate on the story program.
8. Plan to check out books for your child to take the storytime experience home with you. Some books will be in the StoryRoom.
9. You will receive a handout each week that lists books, fingerplays, songs, and rhymes used in the program, and ideas for activities for you and your child to do at home.

Our main goal is for everyone to have a good time. With your help, we can develop and nurture your toddler's love of books and the library. The library staff will be happy to assist you either before or after storytime with selection of books or other library services.

Figure 9. Sample follow-up letter from *Storytimes for Two-Year-Olds*, by Judy Nichols (ALA, 1987), p. 5.
*See comment about use of carpet squares versus carpeting on page 79.

and toddlers, fig. 10.) A typical program might include the following components:

> theme song or music to settle the group (use same each week in a storytime series)
>
> attention-getter, such as the use of a puppet
>
> name song, where everyone is greeted by name by the librarian or the puppet
>
> hand or finger play
>
> story
>
> activity song, rhyme song, circle song
>
> second story
>
> ending song
>
> book sharing, where children and parents or caregivers look at books together

Children less than eighteen months of age are not ready for much story listening in a group, but enjoy interacting with the parents or caregivers in turn-taking games such as "pat-a-cake" and "peek-a-boo," chanting nursery rhymes, singing, and looking at clear, bright pictures. Use Mother Goose and books with pictures of familiar objects and experiences, such as *Goodnight Moon*, by Margaret Wise Brown.

By age two or younger, children are able to follow a simple story plot. As Hannah Nuba has written in "Books and Babies,"

> the age of two is ideal for introducing books to children in a library group setting. By age two, children have developed a strong command of language. They love picture books about familiar experiences, with lilting repetitions and colorful, recognizable illustrations.
>
> Two-year-olds are very concrete in their thinking and not ready to deal with subtle plot lines, abstractions, or fine distinctions. Book experiences for the toddler have until now been mainly on the lap of a caring adult. In the library setting, children still need to see the book close up, page by page, with the librarian occasionally tracing a finger under the text (as parents should do at home) to show the letter-sound-meaning connection.
>
> As the children take their cues from the sounds, the printed symbols on the page, the meaning and enjoyment of the story, the illustrations, and repeated listening experiences, a life-long link between reading and pleasure will have been forged.[3]

Programs centered around a theme are not mandatory, but they do help young children focus and refocus their attention, thus reinforcing learning.

---

3. Hannah Nuba Scheffler, "Books and Babies," in *Infancy: A Guide to Research and Resources*, (New York: Garland, 1986), 145.

1. Hold the storytime in a quiet, carpeted area, away from traffic paths and distractions.
2. Greet the children and their parents and caregivers as they arrive, and give each child a name tag that has been prepared ahead of time.
3. When everyone expected has arrived, take the group to the program area and arrange the group members in a circle with the children on the inside in front of their parents and caregivers. If the program is for infants, most will be lap sitters, but this arrangement will keep infants who have started to crawl or toddlers learning to walk within a safe area.
4. When everyone is seated, greet each child individually by name—you may want to have a puppet companion do this—and welcome all to the library. Some librarians invite the group to join in a welcome song that greets each child by name.
5. Plan to tell from one to three short stories, depending on the age and listening abilities of the children. About fifteen minutes is an appropriate length for the formal part of the program. Select developmentally appropriate books with brief text and clear illustrations.
6. Read the story naturally and unhurriedly. A gentle, quiet voice will encourage the children to listen attentively. Be flexible and willing to accommodate the children's attention span and mood. Remember that the way you present the story will serve as a role model for the parents and caregivers.
7. Young children enjoy hearing the same stories over and over. For a change of pace, you may want to present a flannel board or video version of a book read in a previous week.
8. After the formal part of the program, provide an opportunity for the children to select books on their own from a collection prepared ahead of time. Baskets filled with books are especially inviting. Even babies enjoy crawling to the basket and taking books back to their parents and caregivers for sharing. Hannah Nuba says this activity "helps to reinforce the group experience, extend storytime to individual children and their caregivers, encourage reading-like behavior, and contribute to pre-reading experience in a library environment."
9. Close by thanking everyone for coming—you may want to use your puppet companion again—or have the group sing a good-bye song.
10. Give the parents and caregivers print-outs of the words to the songs and hand and finger plays used in the program. Encourage parents and caregivers to share stories, nursery rhymes, hand and finger plays, and songs at home between the library storytimes. Display parenting books in a prominent place, and encourage browsing.

Figure 10. Storytimes for infants and toddlers—program guidelines for librarians

Children's librarian with monkey puppet in conversation with toddler at Upper Merion Township Library, King of Prussia, Pennsylvania. Photo credit: Barbara Kernaghan.

Judy Nichols' book *Storytimes for Two-Year-Olds* is an excellent resource for program planners and contains thirty-three toddler-tested programs centered on a theme (see fig. 11 for her theme program on bears).[4]

4. Judy Nichols, *Storytimes for Two-Year-Olds* (Chicago: American Library Association, 1987).

Suggested Programs

Bears

Stories Shared

Sleepy Bear
LYDIA DABCOVICH

Ten Bears in My Bed
STANLEY MACK

More Stories to Share at Home

Snow on Bear's Nose
JENNIFER BARTOLI

He Bear, She Bear
STAN BERENSTAIN AND
JAN BERENSTAIN

B Is for Bear
DICK BRUNA

Corduroy
DON FREEMAN

Do Baby Bears Sit in Chairs?
ETHEL KESSLER AND
LEONARD KESSLER

Milton the Early Riser
ROBERT KRAUS

Blueberries for Sal
ROBERT MCCLOSKEY

The Real Mother Goose
MOTHER GOOSE

I'm Going on a Bear Hunt
SANDRA SIVULICH

The Three Bears

Lazy Bear
BRIAN WILDSMITH

Rhythms, Rhymes, and Fingerplays

Bears Everywhere

Bears, bears, bears everywhere (point with index finger)
Bears climbing stairs (make climbing motion)
Bears sitting on chairs (sitting motion)
Bears collecting fares (pretend to accept change)
Bears giving stares (eyes wide open, look around)
Bears washing hairs (rub fingers in hair)
Bears, bears, bears everywhere! (point)

Going on a Bear Hunt

We are going hunting for a bear.
(shade eyes with hand and peer around)
We will walk down the sidewalk;
(pat hands on knees for walking)
Push our way through tall grass;
(alternately push hands away from body side to side)
Swim a river;
(make swimming motions)

Figure 11.   Sample program for toddlers in *Storytimes for Two-Year-Olds,* by Judy Nichols (ALA, 1987), pp. 24-26.

And climb a tall tree.
("climb" as if pulling self up a rope, hands alternating)
Keep looking!!
(shade eyes and peer all around)
What do you see?? A Bear????
(act surprised)
We have to get out of here!
(repeat above motions faster)

Climb down that tree, and Run!
Swim that river, and Run!
Push through that grass, and Run!
Now Run up the sidewalk . . . and in the door . . .
And shut the door tight!
(Clap hands loudly)
Whew . . . I'm glad we are home safe!!
(wipe forehead with fingers and sigh)

Follow-up Ideas

Guess what I am? This guessing game uses the sounds and motions of different animals. Toddlers like to guess, and they like to act out the different animals with you. Start with a picture book about farm animals to give you ideas and to reinforce the actions with a picture. These are also more familiar to your child.

Watch for bears when shopping or when travelling anywhere, look at. magazines and books. This activity is fun since bear logos are plentiful. It helps your toddler become more observant.

Craft

Kitchen Clay

You will need: 2 cups baking soda
1 cup cornstarch
1⅓ cups water
pinch of salt

This recipe feels almost like *real* clay. Put all the ingredients in a saucepan and mix well. Stir over medium heat until the mixture bubbles and thickens. Turn out onto a board or waxed paper and let cool. Knead until smooth. Wrap in a damp towel and place in the refrigerator for 10–15 minutes. Help your child learn how to squeeze, roll, pat, and make balls from clay and to put them together to make many different objects.

Store the clay in a tightly closed plastic bag in the refrigerator, and add a few drops of water to the bag to keep it from hardening. To preserve a special creation, let the object harden in the air for a day or two. Paint with tempera or acrylic paints and cover with shellac. The result: a work of art!

Figure 11. (continued)

Suggested Programs

Program Notes

Opening Routine

Sign   "Bear"—Cross arms over the chest with hands on shoulders. Scratch twice on shoulders.

ST   Book: *Sleepy Bear*

A   "Bears Everywhere" fingerplay

ST   Display book: *Ten Bears in My Bed*. Flannelboard story: Remove ten felt bears on the flannelboard one at a time as you chant or sing the song. Each child can return one of the bears to the flannelboard at the end of the song (or in cooperative groups, let each one take a bear from the flannelboard during the song).

A   Stretching

ST   "Going on a Bear Hunt" action story

P   A bear puppet is "discovered" at the end of the bear hunt. The puppet hugs and is hugged and gives out instructions for quiet time.

QT   Child and parent look at books together.

G   Bear straw caddy

Needed: Pattern enlarged to 4″ hole punch; plastic straw

Copy the pattern and cut out. Punch holes where indicated in top and bottom of bear. Thread straw through. Tape over straw on back if bear slides.

Closing Routine   Bear puppet leads exit from storyspace and says goodbye.

— Notes —

Figure 11.   (continued)

A few librarians have raised the question of how to handle discipline problems. At about eighteen months, toddlers enter a normal stage that psychologists call "negativism." "Why a child has to become ornery and stay that way for a minimum of six to seven months is one of the mysteries that makes the study of early human development so rich and fascinating," writes Burton White in his book *The First Three Years of Life.*[5] During this period, children are acquiring a sense of self and can be remarkably willful. So many things are changing. Perhaps we can understand the two-year-old's wish to control events if we remember how out of control we feel when changes occur in our own lives at a too rapid pace. Warmth, understanding, and a cooperative attitude between the library staff and parents and caregivers is essential for making visits to the library joyous. Occasionally, adults may need to be reminded of what is appropriate behavior in a library setting. Posting rules, such as the guidelines of the New York Public Library's Early Childhood Resource and Information Center (see fig. 12), may be helpful.

Preschool Computer Workshops

A discussion of the pros and cons of introducing computers to young children was presented on pages 47–48. Here are some guidelines by Kate Todd of the New York Public Library for those librarians who would like to offer computer workshops for preschoolers.

1. *Goals and objectives.* The preschool computer workshop is designed to introduce parents and caregivers to software appropriate for young children and to provide enjoyable learning experiences for both parents and caregivers and children.
2. *Age of children.* Children between ages two and five can learn to use the computer if they have developed the manual dexterity to use one finger independently to push one button.
3. *Parental involvement.* The parents and caregivers are expected to sit with their children at the computers to help as needed.
4. *Number of registrants.* Eight to ten children, each accompanied by an adult, is the ideal-size group in order that each child may have a turn at the computer.
5. *Length of series.* A single program can be effective in introducing parents and caregivers to preschool software. A three- or four-session series provides enough training to see preschoolers develop skills at the computer.
6. *Number of software pieces.* Two pieces of software can be introduced in about forty minutes. If librarians offer a series, they may wish to introduce one piece of software at each session in the series.

5. Burton L. White, *The First Three Years of Life*, rev. ed. (New York: Prentice-Hall, 1985), 156–57.

Welcome to the Family Room
Child/Adult Involvement Program

The heart of ECRIC is the Family Room Child/Adult Involvement Program, designed to foster the child's development through close interaction with a caring, supportive adult, i.e., parent or caregiver.

To make your visit a rewarding one, please adhere to the following guidelines:

1) All situations concerning the children must be handled in a quiet, gentle manner. Shouting at children teaches children to shout. Hitting teaches children to hit. *Not permissible here.*

2) The Family Room Program is designed to give you a *special* time with the child in your care—playing with your child, reading to your child, spending interactive quality time together.

   Doing your own thing that *excludes* the child is for another time and place, *not here.*

3) *You must stay close to and supervise your child at all times. Your child's safety is your responsibility.*

4) The Family Room Program is for parents and caregivers with children up to age five only.

5) Parents and caregivers must participate in cleaning up the Family Room Program by returning learning tools, toys, puzzles, etc., to their proper places before leaving.

6) Children are not to be diapered in the Family Room Program. Diaper table is outside Center's door. Diapers must be securely wrapped and discarded in special pail outside the door. Children must not wander outside the Family Room.

7) Snacks are permitted for children only.

8) The Family Room Program is not to be used as a playground, i.e., no running, ball playing, etc., but for gentle, non-disruptive play.

9) Playpens are for infants only.

10) Blocks are to be used only within carpeted areas.

11) Out of consideration for others, do not bring children with sniffles, coughs, rashes, etc., to the Center.

The New York
Public Library

Astor, Lenox and Tilden Foundations
Early Childhood Resource
and Information Center
66 Leroy Street
New York, NY 10014

Figure 12. A sample of the rules developed for ECRIC. A Spanish translation of the rules was also posted.

7. *Vocabulary*. Teach children computer terminology by saying "space bar," "letter M," or "left arrow," instead of "that key." They should also talk about "monitor," "keyboard," and "disc drive" and emphasize the names of different pieces of software.

8. *Clues for success*:

> be completely familiar with the software and the computer before starting their workshop

> set the computer on a trapezoid-shaped table with adjustable metal legs (available from school and office supply companies); set the adjustable legs so that the computer screen is at the child's eye level and the keyboard is at elbow level

> place a chair, without wheels, in front of the computer for the child and another chair for the parent or caregiver

> provide an order, by number or list, so that parents and caregivers will know when their children's turns are coming up

> encourage parents and caregivers to read to their children while waiting to use the computer

> be firm about no food, baby bottles, drinks, or toys in the computer area

> emphasize to parents and caregivers that the workshop should be a *playful* experience for their children.

This picture of a parent/child program at Saratoga Springs (N.Y.) Public Library shows an appropriate seating arrangement. The librarian has opted to use individual cushions on top of the carpeting. Photo credit: Ellen deLalla.

chapter

| 6 |

NETWORKING AND OUTREACH

Networking with Other Child-serving Agencies

One of the most important ways you will spend your time is getting to know the staffs and programs of other child-serving agencies in your community. At the ALSC program "Preschool Services in the Year 2000," presented during the American Library Association's 1990 annual conference in Chicago, Judith Drescher warned children's librarians against isolating themselves with their own constituencies. Drescher, director of the Memphis–Shelby County (Tennessee) Public Library, noted that "the community asking the library director for programming for toddlers is more effective than the children's librarian asking the director for support. . . . The Chamber of Commerce President has more influence on library services than the average parent because business people have the money to fund programs."

Involve your community, and you will multiply your voice. To do this, you will need a profile of each child-serving agency in your community (see fig. 13 for sample form). Keep the profiles in a looseleaf binder to allow for expansion and easy updating.

Consider holding an annual open house for the staffs of these agencies. Your purpose is to increase the agencies' awareness of the library as a basic resource for early childhood materials and services. Display new book and nonbook materials for young children and their parents and caregivers. Talk about the library's services to early childhood. Emphasize the importance of sharing books with young children. Demonstrate techniques of reading aloud, or offer to present a demonstration to agency staff members at a later date. (At one such workshop, the day-care staff confessed they thought reading aloud was boring and hard. After observing the children's librarian reading aloud to a group of two- and three-year-olds, they realized how much fun it could be.) Invite the agencies to display brochures describing their services and to bring some for free distribution to their colleagues. Have a sign-up sheet for agency staff members who would be willing to speak at library programs. Encourage joint planning and implementation.

Name of organization:

Acronym, if used:

Address:

Type of organization (government, private, nonprofit):

Activities and services:

Seasonal activities and services (e.g., summer programs):

Ages served:

Indicate whether agency serves only a particular group (e.g., ethnic, religious):

Hours open: M–F _____   Sat _____   Sun _____

Languages spoken by staff:

Interest in having the librarian give a workshop for staff?

Interest in children's book loan service?

Name, title, and telephone number of contact person:

Date received: _____

Figure 13. Agency profile

A variation of the above approach would be to hold an open house for parents and caregivers and the staffs of child-serving agencies. This would give the parents and caregivers the chance to talk with the staff members of several agencies in one setting, and the agencies the opportunity to publicize their materials and services to a wider audience.

Many libraries hold family reading fairs in collaboration with other child-serving agencies. These feature information booths and mini-workshops for the parents, and films, puppet shows, and hands-on activities for the children or the entire family. To encourage families to visit the library, distribute coupons redeemable for a free children's paperback book upon presentation at the library.

Contact high schools in your community to find out whether any offer parenting programs for teen-age parents or courses in childcare. Offer to present a program to teen-agers on reading aloud to young children. Some of the teen-agers might agree to work as volunteers in read-aloud programs at the library in return for training. The Free Library of Philadelphia started its successful Reading Aloud project in 1985. The staff presents a series of four workshops in which seventh to tenth graders learn criteria for selecting books for reading aloud, techniques of presenting picture books to groups of young children, and program planning. On completion of the course, the young storytellers are presented with certificates and assigned to read aloud at the library, the zoo, schools, or day camps.

Become familiar with the programs and publications of national organizations for child advocacy, such as the National Association for the Education of Young Children (NAEYC), the Children's Defense Fund (CDF), and the National Black Child Development Institute (NBCDI), as well as those of literacy organizations, such as the International Reading Association (IRA) and Reading Is Fundamental (RIF) (see listing on page 106–107). Let the local chapters of these organizations know you are available as a speaker.

Be aware of what is being said and done about services for young children at the local, state, and national levels of government. Let your legislators know what your library is doing for young children and their parents and caregivers. When pertinent bills are being discussed, let your public officials know what this legislation will mean to the parents and children in your community. Participate in state and national conferences. The 1991 White House Conference on Library and Information Service (WHCLIS) offered a unique opportunity to focus on library and informational needs of young children and their parents and caregivers. Make sure children's librarians are represented on ALA Council and on every committee that has any interest in children. At ALA conferences, attend general sessions and meetings outside your own division that have a bearing on children's services.

A few examples of successful collaborations follow.

Beginning with Books

Beginning with Books (BwB) is a nonprofit agency affiliated with the Carnegie Library of Pittsburgh. The initial project was conceived by two

Teen mother and her child during outreach program on reading to children, presented by Beginning with Books, the Carnegie Library of Pittsburgh. Photo credit: Elizabeth Segel.

children's literature specialists, Joan Brest Friedberg and Elizabeth Segel, and funded as a two-year pilot project by small grants from the Pennsylvania Humanities Council and local foundations. (Harper & Row donated 2,000 books.) This early intervention literacy program was directed to 1,000 low-income families enrolled in six Allegheny County (Pennsylvania) Health Department well-baby clinics. A social service worker experienced in counseling met with parents at the clinics to talk about the importance of reading aloud to children in the early years.

Each family filled out a brief questionnaire and received a packet containing four paperback books—*Goodnight Moon*, by Margaret Wise Brown, *Peter's Chair*, by Ezra Jack Keats, *500 Words to Grow On*, illustrated by Harry McNaught, and *Mother Goose*, illustrated by Aurelius Battaglia. The packet also included a pamphlet with tips on reading to young children and a flyer describing local library programs. The initial questionnaire, asking about reading in the home and use of the public library, confirmed that these families rarely used the library. Some of the causes—such as a lack of funds for transportation, anxiety about having to pay for lost or damaged books, unfamiliarity with the library system and procedures, and discomfort with institutions—were expected. What was not expected was comments like "No, we have our own books" and "No, I buy books." Clearly, these families were unaware of the wide range of books and services a public library offers and how such resources could relate to their daily lives.

The families' responses on follow-up questionnaires, used for information and evaluation, showed that the parents appreciated the gift of books, shared them with at least six people, and valued the BwB program, even though 43 percent of the parents themselves had not been read to as children. The Carnegie Library of Pittsburgh also saw the value of the program and offered free office space, financial support, and the use of its resources. In 1986 BwB became an affiliate of the Carnegie Library of Pittsburgh and expanded its program to other community agencies, including hospital outreach clinics, a women's shelter, a child abuse prevention and treatment center, a parental stress center, and community programs for adolescent pregnant women and young single mothers.

Packets in the Gift Book Program now contain three paperback books and a coupon that the family can present at the public library to receive a gift copy of a book (see fig. 14). The three books are chosen by agency personnel from a list of about two dozen titles selected by Friedberg and Segel for their child appeal, literary and artistic merit, and reflection of the cultural experiences of the families served. The books and plastic bags are ordered centrally, but each agency picks up its supply and assembles the individual kits at its offices. Agency personnel who will distribute the packets and counsel parents on the importance of reading aloud are given in-service orientation.

In 1987 BwB initiated a new program called Read Together. One hundred volunteers have since been recruited and trained to read aloud to children age three to ten and to engage them in puzzles, games, and other entertainments

Good for one free book!

Take this coupon to the Children's Room of any branch of

The Carnegie Library of Pittsburgh to receive

a free book for your family.

_____
Branch Library

_____
Agency

Beginning With Books
The Carnegie Library of Pittsburgh, Homewood Branch
7101 Hamilton Avenue, Pittsburgh, PA 15208 412/731-1717

THE CARNEGIE
LIBRARY OF
PITTSBURGH

Figure 14.   Coupon included in the Gift Book Program packet

while their parents are being tutored in literacy. BwB's latest venture is the Read Aloud Parent Club in which Head Start parents meet weekly at a library, where they practice reading aloud children's books within the group before sharing them with their children at home. The parents receive a free book each week and are encouraged to keep a reading journal.

BwB now works with close to thirty agencies and has an advisory board made up of library professionals, child development specialists, a state legislator, school administrators, and representatives from community agencies, corporations, and businesses. Funding comes from local foundations, businesses, individuals, and participating agencies.

BwB has received recognition on national television and in the print media. In 1989 it was featured on "First Things First," a public television special sponsored by Project Literacy U.S. (PLUS). Read Together was one of eight featured in *Family Literacy in Action: A Survey of Successful Programs*.[1] BwB became internationally known when Shirley Biggs of the University of Pittsburgh went as a delegate to the 1985 International Women's Conference in Nairobi and took with her information and materials describing BwB. Many of the delegates expressed interest in the project and felt it could be implemented in their own countries.

An administrative manual is available at a moderate cost to anyone interested in starting a gift book distribution.[2]

Project Leap

The Library's Educational Alternative for Preschoolers—called Project Leap—is Cuyahoga County (Ohio) Public Library's response to the need for quality literature in childcare settings. Through the project, 1,000 storytime kits, 80 puppet shows, and a model 300-title childcare center library have been created. Each storytime kit consists of eight books on specific themes or concepts, such as "pockets" or "being brave," a piece of appropriate realia, a storytime tip sheet, and an audiocassette. For circulation, the materials are packed in sturdy, 15-by-12-by-10-inch bright blue boxes decorated with the LEAP logo (see fig. 15). Materials can be checked out for a week. The eighty puppet show kits contain puppets, props, a written script, and a script recorded on a cassette tape. The puppet shows are the creation of professional puppeteer Rosemary McCormack, who designs and makes all the puppets and props by hand. The puppet shows are organized so that one person can perform them. The core collection of 300 "sustaining books" are available for childcare provider staffs to examine. A booklet of annotations

1. M. Conlon McIvor, ed., Foreword by Ruth S. Nickse, *Family Literacy in Action: A Survey of Successful Programs* (Syracuse, N.Y.: Laubach Literacy International/New Readers Press, 1990). See also Jill L. Locke, "Pittsburgh's Beginning with Books Project," *School Library Journal* 34:6 (February 1988): 22–24.

2. For further information, contact Beginning with Books, Carnegie Library of Pittsburgh, Homewood Branch, 7101 Hamilton Avenue, Pittsburgh, PA 15308, (412) 731-1717.

Figure 15. Logo for Project LEAP

of the books and a discussion of some of the principles of collection development is also available.

Janice Smuda, the project librarian, acts as a resource person for childcare providers, parents, and other librarians by arranging workshops, developing booklists, putting out a quarterly newsletter, and conducting staff training visits at the childcare centers. The workshops are designed to enable childcare providers to make the best possible use of the project materials and to help them recognize the developmental needs and capabilities of preschoolers.[3]

Success by 6 Project

The Minneapolis Public Library and Information Center collaborated with the Minneapolis Health Department to reach 1,500 at-risk families with two-month, six-month, and one-year-old children. Experience has shown that these poverty-born children are at risk of being less developed physically and mentally, and less resilient emotionally, at the time they enter first grade. The project was sponsored by a $15,000 grant from the United Way's "Tools for Success by 6" Committee.

The project's goals are "to encourage parents with low-literacy skills to introduce elements of reading and play in an appropriate manner that stimulates natural literacy and sensory-motor development; to reflect cultural diversity in the materials and methods of communication; and to ensure that the families have the opportunity to know and use the public library." The "tools" to achieve these goals include books, toys, and an eye-catching poster ("Yes You Can! Help your baby be bright and happy") that

3. For further information about Project LEAP, write to Janice Smuda, Project LEAP Librarian, Cuyahoga County Public Library, Parma-Ridge Branch, 5850 Ridge Road, Parma, OH 44129-3199. See also Linda Rome, "Outreach for Preschoolers: Project LEAP," *Wilson Library Bulletin* (October 1989): 39–41.

matches early childhood behavior to books, toys, and activities at three developmental stages (0–6 months, 6–12 months, and 12–18 months). The poster was printed in English, Spanish, and Hmong to meet the needs of the area's multilingual population (see fig. 16).

The library staff selected and ordered culturally and developmentally appropriate books and toys, prepared booklists, and assembled packets that included information about the library, the booklists, and a map of Minneapolis public library locations. Ginger Bush, a librarian in the Children's Services Department and the project manager, gave a literacy development in-service for nurses in the Health Department. The nurses use the packets and the poster as teaching resources. When a family visits the health clinic, a nurse discusses the information in the age-appropriate section of the poster and gives the parent(s) a toy and book pictured on the poster, along with the packet of library materials. An offshoot of the Success by 6 Project was a decision by the United Way to publish a catalog of developmentally appropriate books and toys for distribution to United Way agencies throughout the United States.[4]

Babywise (Howard County Library)

A program of the Howard County Library in Columbia, Maryland, Babywise brings toys and training to caregivers of children under age three. Nearly 50 percent of mothers of young children in Howard County work outside the home. Family day-care homes increased more than 500 percent in the 1980s. To serve the needs of the youngest user population and their caregivers, the Howard County Library hired a full-time early childhood specialist to take responsibility for collection development, service to family day-care providers, service to teen-age parents, and staff training.

The library's collection features a carefully chosen selection of 1,000 toys, including puzzles; puppets; blocks; and musical, ride-on, and jack-in-the-box-type toys. The toy library is a twelve-foot by fourteen-foot area in the middle of the children's department and includes larger toys that do not circulate. Here, parents and children can play together and, if desired, a parent can request a toy advisory session in which a trained staff person observes the child at play and recommends specific toys to encourge the development of new skills and strengthen old ones. Smaller toys, including some battery-operated toys that can be adapted so that children with limited motor ability can operate them by a switch or by a head or foot movement, circulate in drawstring cloth bags, made by volunteers when commercially made ones proved too expensive. Each bag contains the necessary identification and circulation information. A catalog of color photographs of the toys is available at all Howard County libraries and bookmobiles to assist borrowers with selection.

4. For further information, write to Ginger Bush, Manager, Success by 6 Project, Minneapolis Public Library Children's Services Department, 300 Nicollet Mall, Minneapolis, MN 55407, (612) 372-6532.

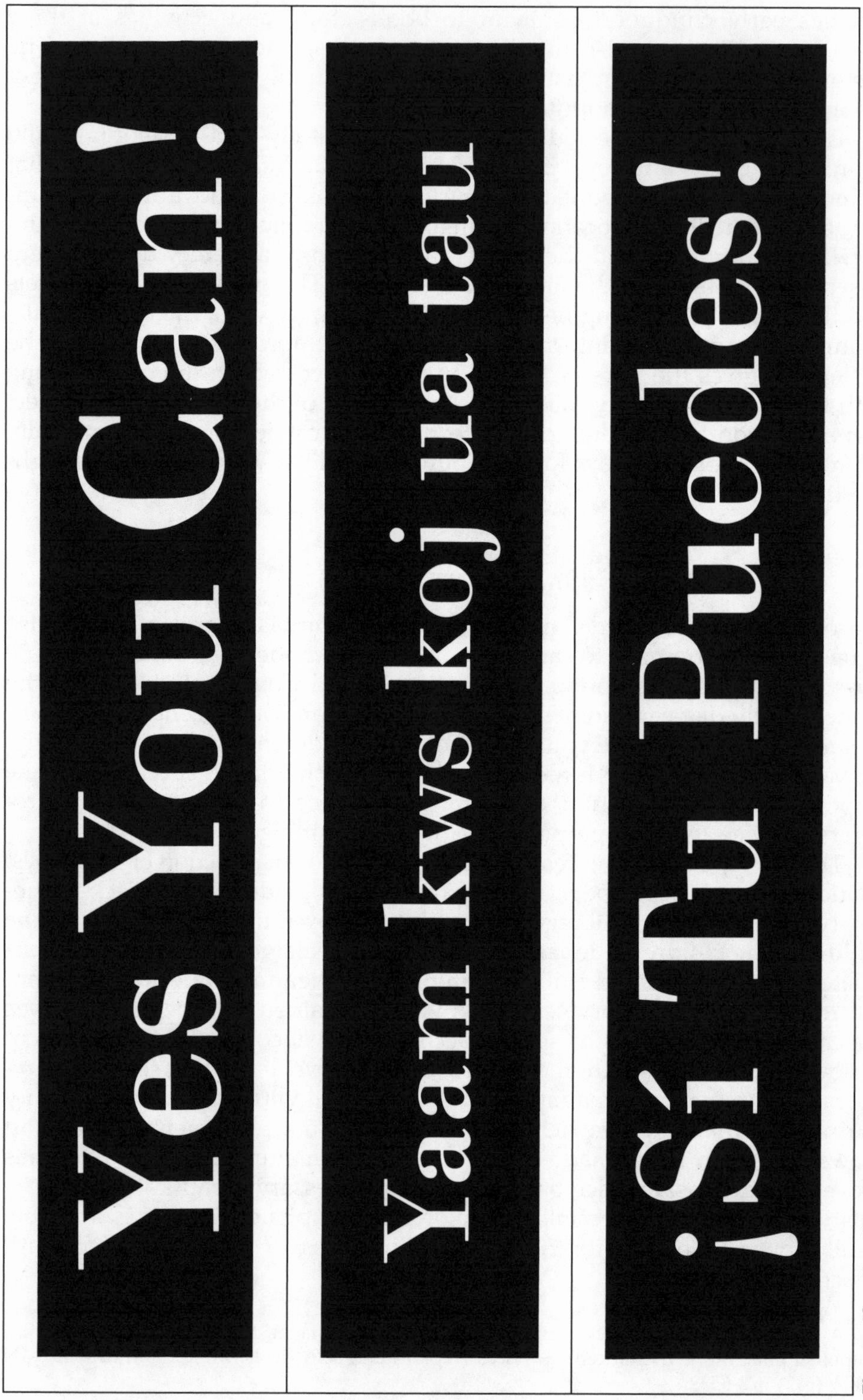

Figure 16. Headlines from Success by 6 Project promotion poster

Day-care kits—teaching units that include books, realia, cassettes, and a manual of suggested activities—deal with topics suggested by the day-care providers and teachers. Storytimes are offered by a library staff member who travels to the day-care homes on a regularly scheduled basis. Special sessions have been offered for parents of infants and toddlers, including a presentation by a pediatrician, a program on time management, an overview of infant CPR, and a workshop on toys as teaching tools.

The early childhood specialist is actively involved in a school system program of education for teen-age parents. In addition, the library conducts a monthly Parent/Child Learning Center that features a resource speaker, toys, books, and a craft activity for children one to three years old. Another program, "Leading to Reading," encourages language development in children eighteen months to two-and-a-half years old. Story programs that feature both toys and books are also offered for the two-and-a-half-year-old child.

Karen Ponish, Babywise's early childhood specialist, has a master's degree in family and child development. Ponish trained the children's librarians in appropriate materials and services for very young children and gave an orientation to the entire library staff to familiarize them with the goals and content of the Babywise program.

Babywise has been cited by the U.S. Department of Education as an exemplary library program. Costs for the program in 1987 included $37,000 for staff and $14,000 for 1,000 toys. The program is funded by a Library Services and Construction Act (LSCA) grant, a two-year grant from the Maryland State Department of Education, and county funds.[5]

Babywise (Nassau Library System)

The Nassau Library System of Uniondale, New York, also has a program called Babywise. The program is designed to reach economically disadvantaged families and to increase literacy and library use by both parents and children. The project is funded through an LSCA grant.

Originally planned for families with children less than two years of age, Babywise expanded in 1989 to reach families with three- and four-year-olds who are enrolled in the county's nine Head Start centers. Ninety percent of the families in the project are below the federal poverty level.

At Babywise Head Start sessions, the librarian talks to the parents and caregivers about the pleasures of reading aloud to preschoolers and presents a sampling of books. Cathleen Towey, Babywise coordinator, described a typical workshop, including titles of books used, in *School Library Journal.*[6] In

5. For further information, write to Babywise Program, Howard County Library, 10375 Little Patuxent Parkway, Columbia, MD 21044, (301) 997-8000, ext. 273. See also Karen Ponish, " 'Babywise' and Toys Develop Literacy Skills," *American Libraries* 18:8 (September 1987): 709–10.

6. Cathleen A. Towey, "Babywise: Booking a Head Start for Parents," *School Library Journal* 36:9 (September 1990): 148–52. For further information, write Cathleen A. Towey, Babywise Coordinator, Nassau Library System, 900 Jerusalem Avenue, Uniondale, NY 11553, (516) 292-8920.

her article, Towey emphasized the importance of discussing the purpose of the workshop with Head Start administrators *before* presenting it and of finding out as much as possible about the parents and children enrolled so that the librarian can present materials and programs that will suit the parents' needs and not overwhelm them with too much information.

At the end of the workshop, each family is presented with a welcome packet to take home. The packet contains a paperback edition of *Goodnight Moon* (books were funded with a neighborhood grant from Chase Manhattan Bank), a brochure about the values of reading aloud, a pamphlet describing materials and programs available at the library, a literacy volunteer's brochure, and a coupon for a second free paperback book that can be picked up at the local library. "Follow-up is crucial," says Towey. "Disadvantaged families spend most of their time simply surviving; it takes time to encourage these families to develop new habits. . . . Librarians should stay in touch with the parents by sending them library newsletters with program information. . .and giving a group tour of the library."

Collaboration between Public Libraries and Universities

Another type of successful collaboration is that between public libraries and universities, such as the New York Public Library and New York University joint sponsorship of an early childhood course and a national conference. In the conference summary session, panelist Carol Millsom, professor of early childhood at New York University, suggested that students in early childhood education and students in library science take courses together as well as field trips together to observe storyhours in preschools and libraries. Millsom believes that students who are trained together will work together. An illustration of this is the program at Shippensburg University in Pennsylvania, where students in early childhood education, under the skillful guidance of Sara Willoughby-Herb and her librarian-husband Steven Herb, conduct or assist in toddler storytimes in public libraries. The sharing that takes place between the students and librarians affects both disciplines and enriches professional relationships in future years.

Outreach to the Homeless

Though homelessness has always been with us, a startling increase in the number of people without a place to live occurred in the 1980s. Several factors have contributed to the situation:

About a half million units of low-income rental housing have been lost every year to cooperative and condominium conversion.

Federally sponsored low-income housing has decreased.

Unemployment has risen.

Government has failed to provide care for much of the mentally ill population.

The constant struggle to survive on the street, in a shelter, or in a welfare hotel leaves the adult with a feeling of hopelessness. For a child living under such appalling conditions, normal development is impossible.

How can the library provide service to people who have no permanent address, no reliable school situation, none of the support systems routinely expected to be available, and no structured environment in which to read and enjoy books? In New York City, librarians have gone into shelters and welfare hotels with picture books to share stories and fingerplays with young children and their parents. Deposit collections of paperback books have been placed in the shelters. Parents and other adults have been directed to the library's community information collection, where they can find sources and agencies to help them with their day-to-day needs—food stamps, day care, housing, advocacy, clothing, health care, and so on.

Librarians who have gone to the shelters to share books and stories warn those who have not worked in such settings to be prepared for chaos. Often, storytimes had to be held in noisy hallways filled with residents who were noticeably distressed. Networking with other agencies is essential. In one neighborhood, all the agencies that provided services to the shelter formed a coalition that met once a month to discuss any problems that arose and to share experiences. A social worker from one of the participating agencies conducted an orientation for the librarians and told them what difficulties they were likely to encounter. Several librarians also attended a series of sensitivity training workshops given by the School of Social Work at Columbia University. The workshops were free and open to people working with the homeless. This sensitivity training proved invaluable.

Once the librarians got used to working in the shelters, they found the programs not very different from those held in the library, except for one significant feature: in the shelters, many school-aged children attended and enjoyed the picture book programs. The children were supposed to be registered in school, but because families were constantly being bumped from one shelter to another, these children fell between the cracks. The librarians welcomed the children and simply began bringing a wider range of books to use in the programs. The children and parents appreciated the library's efforts and loved the stories and books. The New York librarians hope, in time, to stock a bookmobile so they can visit all the shelters regularly.

The problem of homeless people may be with us for some time. Librarians cannot provide homeless people with shelter or food, but if we can mobilize ourselves as a profession, we can, on a modest scale, provide access to books and other library services and perhaps make a difference in their lives.

Outreach to Non-English-speaking Parents and Caregivers

In cities like New York, Los Angeles, Minneapolis, and Miami, and even in smaller suburban communities in the United States today, the population is ethnically and racially diverse, and immigration is continual. Most of the new immigrants come from Mexico, the Philippines, Vietnam, and China.

In multilingual communities, outreach to non-English-speaking parents and caregivers—and other adults learning to read and write in English—has become a vital part of library service.

How can the children's librarian involve non-English-speaking parents and caregivers in literary experiences with their children? Speaking at the NYPL/NYU Early Childhood Conference, Iris R. Sutherland, co-author of *ALERTA: A Multicultural Bilingual Approach to Teaching Young Children*, noted that the early experiences of *all* children depend on their parents.[7] Meeting the needs of non-English-speaking parents entails understanding the cultures involved, learning different customs and family patterns, and acknowledging our commonalities. Accepting the differences among us means that we have to be open and flexible enough to accept people who speak differently than us and to reach out to them.

The importance of the child's mother tongue cannot be emphasized enough, Sutherland stated. To take that away is to deprive a child of a part of himself. Once a child has a frame of reference in his own language, he can readily transfer his skills to learning the second language. Research studies show that the bilingual child learns two languages in much the same way and in the same order as a monolingual child learns one language. The obvious difference is that the bilingual child must be able to distinguish between the two. This ability develops at about age three. At two and a half years of age, there is still some mixture. Experience has shown that as long as parents and caregivers are consistent in their use of the two languages, there are no adverse effects in language development. Children require close relationships, and the use of a familiar language assists in the cognitive and emotional development necessary to build those relationships. Encourage parents and caregivers to use language constantly—for example, to talk with the children about what they are going to wear that day, what they will see on their walk together, and so forth.

The role of books in bilingual language maintenance is important and is recognized by parents who read to their children in each of the languages they know. If librarians believe it is important for parents to read to their children, then we must help them find appropriate reading materials and ways of sharing. The library staff might prepare a video for home use, showing parents how to read aloud and how to talk with young children about the stories shared. The video should be available both in the relevant foreign language and in English.

As the need for children's books in other languages increases, publishers are responding by issuing old favorites in dominant foreign languages, such as the Spanish *Un Dia de Nieve* (*The Snowy Day*), by Ezra Jack Keats, and *Buenos Noches Luna* (*Goodnight Moon*), by Margaret Wise Brown. Isabel Schon, director and professor at the Center for the Study of Books in Spanish for Children and Adolescents, California State University–San

7. R. Leslie Williams et al., with the ALERTA staff, *ALERTA: A Multicultural Bilingual Approach to Teaching Young Children*, Illus. by Jane McCreary (Menlo Park, Calif.: Addison-Wesley, 1985). See also Edith Harding and Philip Riley, *The Bi-Lingual Family: A Handbook for Parents* (New York: Cambridge University Press, 1986).

Marcos, has written extensively about Hispanic books for children and has published a list of notable books in Spanish for the very young.[8] Another helpful bibliography, *Libros en Español para los Pequeños*, selected by the New York Public Library's Libros en Español Committee, may be ordered from the library's Office of Branch Libraries. For distributors of Spanish and other foreign-language books for children, see the list reprinted from *Booklist*, August 1990, on pages 107–12.

Non-English-speaking parents and caregivers who have not yet discovered the library can be reached at clinics, grocery stores, Laundromats, churches, and the workplace. Booklists and informational flyers about library programs and services to be distributed at these gathering places should be in bilingual format.

At the New York Public Library's Centers for Reading and Writing (CRW), adults age sixteen and older can receive individual and group instruction in becoming literate in English (whether or not English is a second language). Librarians in the NYPL/NYU early childhood course quickly discovered a natural tie-in with the CRW program: Many of the adults in the CRW programs are parents or grandparents. Because they already want to read to their children and help them with their homework, they are highly motivated to learn to read for themselves. One literacy student wrote, "I am a woman, 28, and have a new baby girl. I want to learn to read so that I can read stories to her when she's older. I will be very ashamed if she finds out that I can't read."

This mother and others like her can improve their reading skills while enjoying books with their children. Wordless picture books, because they offer opportunities to explore language together without requiring proficiency in reading, are a good starting point. Examples include *Sunshine* and *Moonlight*, by Jan Ormerod; Raymond Briggs' *The Snowman*; *Changes, Changes*, by Pat Hutchins; and *Up a Tree*, by Ed Young.

Another approach is for parents and caregivers and their children to make books together, using pictures from old magazines or greeting cards, and make up stories about the people, scenes, and objects in the pictures. They can use family photographs to relate true stories about family members, relatives, and special occasions. There are several good intergenerational books now available, such as *Basket*, by George Ella Lyon, and *When I Am Old with You*, by Angela Johnson, that might serve as catalysts for parents or grandparents to share a part of their own personal histories with their offspring.

Both the American Association of Retired Persons and the Child Welfare League of America sponsor intergenerational childcare programs. Addresses of both groups are in the appendix following.

8. Isabel Schon, "Recent Notable Books in Spanish for the Very Young," *Journal of Youth Services in Libraries* 2:2 (Winter 1989): 162–164. See also Schon and Betty Greathouse, "Valuing Diversity: The Role of Developmentally Appropriate Books in Spanish," *Childhood Education* 66:5 (Annual theme issue 1990): 311–15.

Appendixes
Pertinent Resource Centers and Organizations

Here are listed 25 resources for professionals who work with very young children and their parents and caregivers.

Action for Children's Television (ACT)
20 University Road
Cambridge, MA 02138

American Association of Retired
  Persons (AARP)
3200 E. Carson Street
Lakewood, CA 90712

American Library Association
Association for Library Service to
  Children (ALSC)
50 E. Huron Street
Chicago, IL 60611

Association for Childhood Education
  International (ACEI)
11141 Georgia Avenue
Suite 200
Wheaton, MD 20902

Center for Children's Media
451 W. Broadway
New York, NY 10012-3156

Center for Parent Education
55 Chapel Street
Newton, MA 02160

Child Welfare League of America
Generations United
440 First Street, NW
Suite 310
Washington, DC 20001-2085

Children's Defense Fund (CDF)
112 C Street, NW
Washington, DC 20001

Consortium of Family Organizations
  (COFO)
c/o Family Policy Report
1319 F Street NW, Suite 606
Washington, DC 20004

Day Care Council of America
711 14th Street NW, Suite 507
Washington, DC 20005

The Epicenter, Inc.
"The Education for Parenthood
  Information Center"
15 Bemis Road
Wellesley Hills, MA 02181

ERIC Clearinghouse on Elementary
  and Early Childhood
  Education
555 New Jersey Avenue, NW
Washington, DC 20208

ERIC Clearinghouse on
  Handicapped and Gifted
  Children
Council for Exceptional Children
1920 Association Drive
Reston, VA 22091

High/Scope Educational Research
  Foundation
600 N. River Street
Ypsilanti, MI 48197

International Reading Association
  (IRA)
800 Barksdale Road
P.O. Box 8139
Newark, DE 19714-8139

National Association for Gifted
  Children
8080 Springvalley Drive
Cincinnati, OH 45236

National Association for the
  Education of Young Children
  (NAEYC)
1834 Connecticut Avenue, NW
Washington, DC 20009

National Black Child Development
Institute
1463 Rhode Island Avenue, NW
Washington, DC 20005

National Center for the Prevention
and Treatment of Child Abuse
and Neglect
1205 Oneida Street
Denver, CO 80220

National Clearinghouse for Bilingual
Education
1300 Wilson Boulevard
Rosslyn, VA 22209

National Council for Children's
Rights, Inc.
721 2nd Street NE
Washington, DC 20002

New York Public Library
Early Childhood Resource and
Information Center (ECRIC)
66 Leroy Street
New York, NY 10012

Reading Is Fundamental (RIF)
Smithsonian Institution
P.O. Box 23444
Washington, DC 20026

USA Toy Library Association
104 Wilmot Road
Suite 201
Deerfield, IL 60015

U.S. Office of Education
Parent/Early Childhood Education
400 Maryland Avenue, SW
Washington, DC 20202

Distributors of Children's Foreign-Language Books: Update 1990

Under the auspices of the ALA ALSC Committee on the Selection of Children's Books and Materials from Various Cultures, who prepare annotated bibliographies for *Booklist*, this list of distributors who regularly provide children's books in languages other than English has been revised and expanded by Diane Holzheimer, librarian, Tenacre School, Wellesley, Mass. First published in *Booklist* on August 1981 and now appearing every 18 months, the compilation reflects the substantial increase in the number of companies who furnish these materials as well as the recent expansion of the committee charge to include English-language materials originating in other countries. The information results from a survey of vendors listed in the last revision, suppliers of children's and adult materials of foreign language bibliographies that have appeared in *Booklist*, booksellers who contacted the committee, and other recently identified distributors.

By Distributor

Adler's Foreign Books
915 Foster St.
Evanston, IL 60201-3199
French, German, Spanish
(Mexico, Argentina)

AIMS International
Books
3216 Montana Ave.
P.O. Box 11496
Cincinnati, OH 45211
Spanish (Mexico, Spain,
Venezuela, Argentina,
Chile, U.S.)

Almeda County Office
of Education
Publication Sales
313 W. Winton Ave.
Hayward, CA
94544-1198
Vietnamese

Albert J. Phiebig Inc.
Services to Libraries
P.O. Box 352
White Plains, NY
10602-0352
Spanish (all countries)

Arte Publico Press
University of Houston
4800 Calhoun, 2-L
Houston, TX 77204-2090
Spanish (Argentina,
Spain)

Astran Inc.
7965 N.W. 64th St.
Miami, FL 33166
Spanish (Spain, Mexico,
Argentina)

Australian Book Source
1309 Redwood Ln.
Davis, CA 95616
Australian

Bernard H. Hamel
Spanish Books
2326 Westwood Blvd.
Los Angeles, CA 90064
Spanish (all countries)

Bilingual Publications
Company
270 Lafayette St., Ste.
705
New York, NY 10012
Spanish (Spain, Latin
America, Canada,
U.S.)

Children's Book Press
1339 61st St.
Emeryville, CA 94608
Korean, Vietnamese,
Spanish (Mexico,
Nicaragua, Puerto Rico,
El Salvador)

Children's Book Store
604 Markham St.
Toronto, Ontario M6G
2L8
French, Bengali, Chinese,
Hindi

China Cultural Center
Inc.
970 N. Broadway, #210
Los Angeles, CA 90012
Chinese

Claudia's Caravan
P.O. Box 1582
Almeda, CA 94501
Spanish (Spain, Mexico),
French, Vietnamese,
Hmong, Lao, Korean,
Arabic, Japanese,
Navajo

Croatian Books
6313 St. Clair Ave.
Cleveland, OH 44103
Croatian

Donar's Spanish Books
P.O. Box 24
Loveland, CO
80539-0024
Spanish (Spain, Mexico,
Venezuela, Peru)

Downtown Book
Center Inc.
247 S.E. 1st St.
Miami, FL 33131
Spanish (Spain, Latin
America)

Editions Champlain
107 Church St.
Toronto, Ontario
Canada M5C 2G5
French

Editorial de la
Universidad de
Puerto Rico
Apartado 23322
San Juan, Puerto Rico
00931-3322
Spanish (Spain, Latin
America)

Encyclopaedia
Britannica
Educational
Corporation
310 S. Michigan Ave.
Chicago, IL 60604
Spanish, French, Arabic

European Book Co.
925 Larkin St.
San Francisco, CA
94109
French, German, Spanish
(Spain, Argentina)

Evergreen Publishing
& Stationery
136 S. Atlantic Blvd.
Monterey Park, CA
91754
Chinese

Far Eastern Books
P.O. Box 846
Adelaide St. Station
Toronto, Canada M5C
2K1
Bengali, Gujarati, Hindi,
Punjabi, Urdu,
Marathi, Tamil (India,
Pakistan, Sri Lanka,
Bangladesh)

Fiesta Publishing Corp.
6360 N.E. 4th Ct.
Miami, FL 33138
Spanish

**French & Spanish
Book Corp.**
115 Fifth Ave.
New York, NY
10003-9931
*French (France,
Switzerland, Belgium),
Spanish (Spain, Mexico,
Puerto Rico, Argentina)*

Gerald J. Fuchs
1841 Broadway, #904
New York, NY 10023
German

Gererd Hamon, Inc.
P.O. Box 758
Mamaroneck, NY 10543
French, Spanish, German

Haitian Book Center
P.O. Box 324
Flushing, NY
11369-0324
French, Haitian Creole

**Hispanic Books
Distributors, Inc.**
1665 W. Grant Rd.
Tucson, AZ 85745
*Spanish (Mexico, Spain,
Argentina, Venezuela)*

**Hispanic Information
Exchange**
16161 Ventura Blvd.,
#830
Encino, CA 91436
*Spanish (Mexico, Spain,
Central America, Latin
America, U.S.)*

Iaconi Book Imports
1110 Mariposa
San Francisco, CA
94107
*Spanish (Mexico,
Nicaragua, Spain,
Venezuela, Argentina,
Peru)*

Imported Books
P.O. Box 4414
2025 W. Clarendon
Dallas, TX 75208
Forty languages,
including
*Arabic, Chinese, French,
German, Italian,
Japanese, Portuguese,
Vietnamese, Spanish
(Mexico, Spain,
Argentina)*

**International Book
Centre**
P.O. Box 295
Troy, MI 48099
*Arabic, Persian, Turkish,
French, Japanese,
Korean, Vietnamese,
Spanish*

**International Book
Import Service, Inc.**
2995 Wall Triana Hwy.,
Ste. B4
Huntsville, AL
35824-1532
German

**James Bennett Library
Services**
8667 Mariners Dr., #28
Stockton, CA 95209
English (Australian)

**Jean Touzot
Libraire-Editeur**
38 rue Saint-Sulpice
75278 Paris Cedex 06
France
French

**Jeong-Eum-Sa Imports
(Korean Book
Center)**
3030 W. Olympic Blvd.,
#111
Los Angeles, CA 90006
Korean

**Kinokuniya Bookstores
of America**
1581 Webster St.
San Francisco, CA
94115
Japanese

Koryo Books Importing
7 W. 32nd St.
New York, NY 10001
Korean

Lectorum Publications
137 W. 14th St.
New York, NY 10011
*Spanish (Spain, Mexico,
Central America, the
Caribbean, South
America, U.S.)*

**Literal Book
Distributors**
1836 Metzerott Rd.,
#1126
Adelphi, MD 20783
*Spanish (Spain, Mexico,
Peru)*

**LTO/Libros! Libros!
Libros!**
1507 Francisco West
San Francisco, CA
94123
Spanish

MACH
Apartado Postal 13-319
03500 Mexico, D.F.
Spanish

Mary S. Rosenberg
1841 Broadway
New York, NY 10023
German

Mazda Publishers
P.O. Box 2603
Costa Mesa, CA 92626
Persian

Mladost
37 Creekwood Dr.
West Hill, Ontario,
  Canada M1E 4L6
Croatian, Macedonian,
  Serbo-Croatian,
  Slovenian, Serbian

National Hispanic
  University
255 E. 14th St.
Oakland, CA 94606
Cambodian, Chinese,
  Filipino, Punjabi,
  Spanish, Vietnamese

Nedbook International
  b-v.
P.O. Box 3113
1003 AC Amsterdam,
  The Netherlands
Dutch

NTC Publishing Group
4255 W. Touhy Ave.
Lincolnwood (Chicago),
  IL 60646
Spanish, French,
  German, Italian,
  Japanese

Olgerts Dikis
6571 Clines Chapel Rd.
Waverly, OH 45690
Latvian

Pan American Book
  Co., Inc.
4362 Melrose Ave.
Los Angeles, CA 90029
Chinese, English, French,
  German, Italian,
  Spanish, Vietnamese

Pan Asian Publications
  Inc.
P.O. Box 131
Agincourt Stn.
Scarborough, Ontario,
  Canada M1S 3B4
Chinese, Japanese, Khmer,
  Korean, Thai,
  Vietnamese, Lao,
  Tagalog

Pannonia Books
P.O. Box 1017
Postal St. B
Toronto, Ontario,
  Canada M5T 2T8
Hungarian

Polonia Bookstore
2886 N. Milwaukee
  Ave.
Chicago, IL 60618
Polish

Powell's Books
  School/Library
  Services
1005 W. Burnside
Portland, OR 97209
Spanish (Mexico, Central
  America, Spain),
  French, German

Puski-Corvin
251 E. 82nd St.
New York, NY 10028
Hungarian

Puvill Libros
Boters 10, 08002
Barcelona, Spain
Portuguese, Spanish
  (Spain, Mexico, South
  America)

Rashid Sales
191 Atlantic Ave.
Brooklyn, NY 11201
Arabic (Egypt, Lebanon)

S. F. Vanni
30 W. 12th St.
New York, NY 10011
Italian

Schoenof's Foreign
  Books
76A Mount Auburn St.
Cambridge, MA 02138
French, German, Italian,
  Russian, Portuguese,
  Polish (Latin America,
  Scandinavia, Eastern
  Europe, Greece, Israel,
  Far East)

Scott, Foresman and
  Company
1900 E. Lake Ave.
Glenview, IL 60025
Spanish (Mexico, Spain,
  Colombia)

Sefer Israel, Inc.
150 W. 26th St.
Rm. 401
New York, NY 10001
Hebrew

Shen's Books and
  Supplies
628 E. Pamela Rd.
Arcadia, CA 91006
Chinese, Japanese,
  Korean, Vietnamese

Spanish & European
  Bookstore
3117 Wilshire Blvd.
Los Angeles, CA 90010
Spanish (Mexico, Spain,
  Argentina, U.S.)

Speedimpex
45-45 39th St.
Long Island City, NY
  11104
Italian, Spanish

Speelman's Bookhouse
5010 Steeles Ave., W.
 Unit 12
Rexdale, Ontario,
 Canada M9V 5C6
Dutch

**Superanado, S.A. de
 C.V.**
Rio Danubio, #79
Colonia Cuauhtemoc,
 06500, Mexico
Spanish

Tundra Books
1434 St. Catherine St.,
 West #303
Montreal, Quebec,
 Canada H3G 1R4
French

**United Nations-
 Publications
Sales Section**
RM DC2-853
United Nations
New York, NY 10017
French, Spanish

Van Khoa Books
9200 Bolsa Ave.
Ste. 123
Westminster, CA 92683
Vietnamese

Victor Kamkin
4950-56 Boiling Brook
 Pkwy.
Rockville, MD 20852
Russian

Vietnamese Book Store
P.O. Box 97
Los Alamitos, CA 90720
Vietnamese

Workman's Circle
attn. Stephen Dowling
45 E. 33rd St.
New York, NY 10016
*Yiddish, English, Judaica,
 Hebrew, Russian*

Zieleks Co.
11215 Sageland Dr.
Houston, TX 77089
Vietnamese

By Language

Arabic:
Claudia's Caravan;
 Encyclopaedia
 Britannica; Imported
 Books; Int'l Book
 Centre; Rashid

Australian:
Australian Book Source;
 James Bennett

Bengali:
Children's Book Store;
 Far Eastern

Cambodian:
Nat'l Hispanic Univ.

Chinese:
Children's Book Store;
 China Cultural
 Center; Evergreen;
 Imported Books;
 Nat'l Hispanic Univ.;
 Pan American; Pan
 Asian Publications;
 Shen's

Croatian:
Croatian Books;
 Mladost

Dutch:
 Nedbook; Speelman's

Filipino:
Nat'l Hispanic Univ.

French:
Adler's; Children's Book
 Store; Claudia's
 Caravan; Editions
 Champlain;
 Encyclopaedia
 Britannica; European
 Book; French &
 Spanish Book; Gererd
 Hamon; Haitian Book
 Center; Imported
 Books; Int'l Book
 Centre; Jean Touzot;
 NTC Publishing; Pan
 American; Powell's;
 Schoenof's; Tundra
 Books; United
 Nations

German:
Adler's; European Book;
 Gerald J. Fuchs;
 Gererd Hamon;
 Imported Books; Int'l
 Book Import Service;
 Mary S. Rosenberg;
 NTC Publishing; Pan
 American; Powell's;
 Schoenof's

Gujarati:
Far Eastern

Haitian Creole:
Haitian Book Center

Hebrew:
Sefer Israel; Workman's
 Circle

Hindi:
Children's Book Store;
 Far Eastern

Hmong:
Claudia's Caravan

Hungarian:
Pannonia; Puski-Corvin

Italian:
Imported Books; NTC
Publishing; Pan
American; S. F.
Vanni; Schoenof's;
Speedimpex

Japanese:
Claudia's Caravan;
Imported Books; Int'l
Book Centre;
Kinokuniya; NTC
Publishing; Pan
Asian Publications;
Shen's

Khmer:
Pan Asian Publications

Korean:
Children's Book Press;
Claudia's Caravan;
Int'l Book Centre;
Jeong-Eum-Sa
Imports (Korean
Book Center); Koryo
Books; Pan Asian
Publications; Shen's

Lao:
Claudia's Caravan; Pan
Asian Publications

Latvian:
Olgerts Dikis

Macedonian:
Mladost

Marathi:
Far Eastern

Navajo:
Claudia's Caravan

Persian:
Int'l Book Centre;
Mazda

Polish:
Polonia; Schoenof's

Portuguese:
Imported Books;
Schoenof's; Puvill
Libros

Punjabi:
Far Eastern; Nat'l
Hispanic Univ.

Russian:
Schoenof's; Victor
Kamkin; Workman's
Circle

Serbian:
Mladost

Serbo-Croatian:
Mladost

Slovenian:
Mladost

Spanish:
Adler's; AIMS Int'l;
Albert J. Phiebig; Arte
Publico; Astran;
Bernard H. Hamel;
Bilingual Publications;
Children's Book Press;
Claudia's Caravan;
Donar's; Downtown
Book Center; Editorial
de la Universidad de
Puerto Rico;
Encyclopaedia
Britannica; European
Book; Fiesta
Publishing; French &
Spanish Book; Gererd
Hamon; Hispanic
Books; Hispanic
Information
Exchange; Iaconi;
Imported Books; Int'l
Book Centre;
Lectorum; Literal
Book; LTO/Libros!

Libros! Libros!;
MACH; Nat'l
Hispanic Univ.; NTC
Publishing; Pan
American; Powell's;
Puvill Libros;
Schoenof's; Scott,
Foresman; Spanish &
European Bookstore;
Speedimpex;
Superanado; United
Nations

Tagalog:
Pan Asian Publications

Tamil:
Far Eastern

Thai:
Pan Asian Publications

Turkish:
Int'l Book Centre

Urdu:
Far Eastern

Vietnamese:
Alameda County Office
of Education;
Children's Book
Press; Claudia's
Caravan; Imported
Books; Int'l Book
Centre; Nat'l
Hispanic Univ.; Pan
American; Pan Asian
Publications; Shen's;
Van Khoa;
Vietnamese Book
Store; Zieleks

Yiddish:
Workman's Circle

chapter

7

PLANNING, IMPLEMENTING, AND EVALUATING LIBRARY SERVICE TO EARLY CHILDHOOD

A program of service encompasses staff, materials, programs, physical facilities, and evaluation. Service to early childhood, perhaps more so than service to any other group, involves all departments in the library—adult, young adult, children's, outreach, technical services, public relations, and others. Take this opportunity to *jointly* plan, develop, and implement service to the youngest library users and their parents and caregivers.

Steps in Planning

1. Establish a profile of your branch library community (see fig. 17 for sample form).
2. Assess your community's needs in the area of early childhood. Listen to community service workers—for example, social service program directors, Head Start teachers, public health workers, clergy, and so on. Most importantly, ask parents and other caregivers what they need. Note that each of the model centers described in chapter 1 was the result of a formal study of preschoolers' public library needs, of informal discussions with parents and community child caregivers, or of an advisory committee composed of parents and professionals working with young children.
3. Develop a clear statement of your goals and objectives. Goals, as defined in *Planning and Role Setting for Public Libraries*, "are long-range and represent a vision of excellence in library service. Objectives are specific, time limited, and measurable or verifiable."[1] In other words, what do you want to accomplish? Determine priorities by selecting the needs, interests, and problems you wish to address. (Priorities represent the order of precedence assigned to the goals and objectives derived from the needs assessment.)

1. Charles R. McClure et al., *Planning and Role Setting for Public Libraries: A Manual of Options and Procedures* (Chicago: American Library Association, 1987), 3.

Community Profile Form

Demographic Characteristics

Total population:

Population under age 3:

Number of households:

Number of families:

Percentage of families below poverty level:

Ethnicity (Note percentage of total population for each group.)

African-American:

Asian-American:

European-American:

Hispanic-American:

Cuban:

Mexican:

Puerto Rican:

Other:

Native American or Inuit:

Other:

Give a brief history of the community, including cultures represented, languages spoken, local politics, major businesses and industries, housing facilities, hospitals, social service agencies, day-care centers, schools, colleges, and universities, churches, museums, recreational facilities, and so on.

Briefly describe the community's present needs, strengths, interests, and problems.

What are the community's plans for the future? How might these factors affect library service to early childhood?

Figure 17. A sample community profile form for the community the library serves

4. Specify a time frame. Long-range goals and objectives are what you hope to accomplish within a three- to five-year period. Short-range goals and objectives are what you think you can accomplish within one to two years or less.
5. List the library's present services for young children (birth to age three) and their parents and caregivers.
6. List your resources.
7. List any constraints to accomplishing your objectives.
8. Estimate the cost of what you want to do (see the following section on budgeting).
9. Discuss your plans and budget with your supervising librarian or library director. Resolve any disagreements on goals, objectives, or process *before* proceeding.
10. Develop, compare, and select optional strategies (methods to be transformed into actions).
    a. Make a list of all options that will help you to achieve the specific objectives.
    b. For each option, consider the factors necessary to implement the option.
    c. Evaluate each option against the goals and objectives and compare the results.
    d. Select the best option.
    e. Implement the strategies.
    f. Coordinate plans with other specialities within your library. Plug into existing library programs, such as English as a second language (ESL), centers for reading and writing (CRW), or other literacy programs.
    g. Network with other child-centered agencies in your branch library community.

One of the best tools available for planning, measuring, and evaluating a service program is the previously mentioned publication *Planning and Role Setting for Public Libraries*. Its authors outline eight basic roles for libraries, ranging from community activities center to research center. No library has the resources to fulfill all roles, so each library must select primary, secondary, and maintenance roles. One to two roles are recommended as primary, one to two as secondary, and the remainder as maintenance. Of the eight roles discussed, Preschoolers' Door to Learning is the one of direct interest to the readers of this book (see fig. 18). The manual is replete with sensible advice and a number of workforms. As such, it is highly recommended reading.

Budget

To estimate the cost of early childhood service, distinguish between the initial cost of setting up the service and ongoing costs.

Preschoolers' Door to Learning

DESCRIPTION: The library encourages young children to develop an interest in reading and learning through services for children, and for parents and children together. Parents and other adult caregivers can locate materials on reading readiness, parenting, child care, and child development. Cooperation with other child care agencies in the community is ongoing.

The library promotes reading readiness from infancy, providing services for self-enrichment and for discovering the pleasures of reading and learning. Services may include programs for infants, for parents and toddlers, and for parents—for example, "read-aloud," day-care story hour, traditional storytelling, parenting skills development workshops, and booktalks. The library may provide outreach to day-care facilities, or reading readiness programs. Programming introduces children and adults concerned with children to a wide range of materials and formats.

BENEFITS: Preschoolers have a place designed for their needs with trained adults to help them satisfy their curiosity, stimulate new interests, and find information. They become familiar with library materials in a variety of formats and develop reading, listening, viewing, and thinking skills. Parents can obtain resources and services to support their efforts to develop their children's interests, experience, knowledge, and development.

For the community, the library promotes early reading and acceptance of reading, factors contributing to successful performance in formal schooling. This role promotes lifelong use of the library and contributes to the library's image as an educational center for individuals of all ages. This role generates visibility, popularity, and support for the library in the community by reaching children unserved by any other community agency. In addition, services for children are popular with voters.

CRITICAL RESOURCES: *The collection* has a variety of materials and formats for preschoolers and for adults working with young children. Some libraries provide computers, audiovisual formats, educational toys, and games to help children expand their imagination and develop motor and sensory skills. Popular titles are available in multiple copies.

The staff are knowledgeable about early childhood development and children's litera-

ture and promote reading readiness to the community. They guide children's choices of books and other materials and are skilled in planning and conducting programs.

The facility is in a location easily accessible to young children. Ample, inviting space is available for programs and story hours. Shelving and furnishings are attractive, accessible, and comfortable for young children.

OUTPUT MEASURES TO EXPLORE: (Use the percent of the population under 5 for per capita measures. For turnover rate, use only the portion of the collection intended for use by preschoolers, such as picture books and audiovisual materials.)

• Circulation per Capita
• Library Visits per Capita
• Program Attendance per Capita
• Turnover Rate.

Figure 18. Preschoolers' Door to Learning from *Planning and Role Setting for Public Libraries: A Manual of Options and Procedures,* by Charles R. McClure et al. (ALA, 1987), p. 37.

Initial Costs

1. Room set-up

    carpeting for the area set aside for early childhood activities

    a few comfortable chairs for lap reading (Both adults and children enjoy overstuffed chairs and large rockers.)

    shelving for picture books

    specially designed bookcases to hold cloth and board books

    hangers for book and cassette kits

    shelving for a basic parenting collection, including books and periodicals

    shelving for computer software and videos

    storage cabinets for toys, flannel board, puppets, etc.

2. Materials

    cloth books (examples to show parents)

    board books

    picture books

    realia, including toys, puppets, flannel board, and flannel board figures

    computer software

    films and videos

    cassettes

    parenting collection and vertical file.

3. Staff training time

Ongoing Costs

1. Staff time—professional librarian and assistants
2. Materials (book and nonbook; replacement and new additions)
3. Arts and crafts materials
4. Honoraria and expenses for guest presenters
5. Flyers and posters
6. Postage and mailing costs
7. Telephone

Staff/Training

Staffing early childhood services requires a professional librarian and support staff. The ideal education for a librarian, according to librarians working in this area, is a joint degree in librarianship and early childhood education. Next best is a degree in librarianship with courses in early childhood development. Surveys by Bernice Cullinan and me and by Frances Smardo indicate that most library schools currently do not offer courses specifically designed to prepare librarians to work with young children and their parents.[2] As a result, public libraries that select the Preschoolers' Door to Learning role will need to develop an in-service training program in this area.

In the last chapter, you read about Howard County Library's decision to hire a person with a master's degree in family and child development to direct early childhood services and train the staff. Here are two more examples of successful in-service programs.

The New York Public Library Early Childhood Resource and Information Center (ECRIC) serves as a resource for staff development. Librarians in the system who will be working extensively in early childhood services spend time at ECRIC observing parent-child interaction in the Family Room, listening to lectures by early childhood specialists, getting to know the collections (including the vertical file), and participating in floor work under the guidance of ECRIC's director, Hannah Nuba.

At the branch level, Steve del Vecchio, one of the participants in the NYPL/NYU course (see outline in Appendix B), developed an informal educational program for the staff of the Aguilar branch. This project resulted from the staff's response to del Vecchio's enthusiastic description of the classes. He shared the course readings and gleanings from the guest lecturers and encouraged staff members to pursue their own reading interests in this area. Several staff members had young children of their own and were deeply interested in the subject from a personal point of view. They openly shared their feelings and thoughts about books in the parenting collection. They were eager to try out picture books and toys with their infants and toddlers and report back to the group on the children's responses. When I visited the branch to observe a toddler storytime, I was struck by the warm feeling between the staff and the mothers and toddlers. This positive tone makes for excellent service and, in turn, good community support for the library.

Another successful training program was Connecticut's "Beginnings— Public Library Services for Two-Year-Olds and Their Parents," directed by Frank Self, a professor at St. Joseph College in West Hartford. The originator of and consultant for the project was Faith H. Hektoen, consultant at the Connecticut State Library. Nancy De Salvo, coordinator of services to children and young adults at the Farmington Library, was program assistant. The training program was funded by a Library Services Construction Act (LSCA) grant.

Self described the program as follows:

> "Beginnings" is a parenting program to help parents extend their ideas and develop their skills. It helps parents extend their ideas about play with their very young children. It helps parents develop their skills in playing with their very young children....To facilitate this parenting

2. Ellin Greene and Bernice E. Cullinan, "Educating Librarians to Serve Early Childhood," *School Library Journal* 34:11 (August 1988): 54; Frances A. Smardo, "Are Librarians Prepared to Serve Young Children?" *Journal of Education for Librarianship* 20:4 (Spring 1980): 274–84.

program, children's librarians must also extend and develop their actual knowledge, ideas, and skills. They must extend their ideas about the development of very young children, about library programs involving very young children, and also about their role vis-à-vis children and parents in those programs. And, of course, they must develop their skills in helping parents to play with their children.[3]

Sixty-six children's librarians in Connecticut participated in the training program. To help them develop their skills, Self wrote a manual and presented three training seminars consisting of four sessions each. A fifth session, involving all the participants, followed the seminars. As a result of the two-year project, sixty-two children's rooms in Connecticut libraries have parent resource collections and offer parent support programs. In evaluating the Beginnings program, the children's librarians said they felt more confident about working with young children and about developing quality programs for them. Their viewpoint about library services broadened as they increasingly saw themselves in the role of parent support.

Use of Volunteers

Many libraries use volunteers in their early childhood programs. If you decide to use volunteers, choose appropriate assignments for them and follow through with training and supervision. The results can be an unexpected bonus. For instance, two of the volunteers in the Parent/Child Workshop program at the Middle Country (New York) Public Library decided to pursue graduate degrees in library work with children. The children's librarian at the Gloucester City (New Jersey) Public Library gave workshops for teen-age parents in the Gloucester City Junior-Senior High School on reading aloud to young children. In addition to sharing books with their own children at home, these young parents now work as volunteers, reading aloud at the library, in kindergarten classes, and to neighborhood children. Retired persons may be persuaded to read aloud to young children in the library on a regular basis or to assist with crafts activities in the toddler storytime. Intergenerational activities, such as the Grandreading project conducted by the Wayne County Library System in Newark, New York,[4] have proven successful.

Designing Library Space

Whenever possible, provide a designated space for young children and their parents and caregivers to interact away from the traffic flow of the room. If the library has a separate meeting room, that space can be adapted for early

3. Frank Self, "Beginnings," in-house training manual, 1979.
4. Nancy M. Rubery, "Practically Speaking: A Grand Idea," *School Library Journal* 36:1 (January 1990): 42.

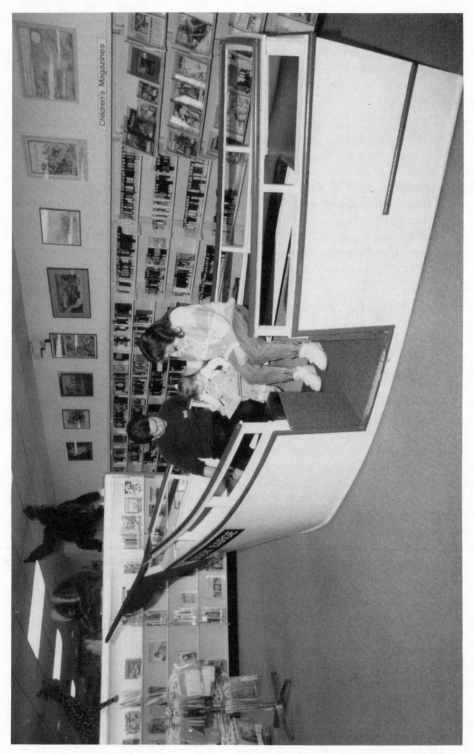

A "boat" provides a quiet space for reading and dreaming in the Middle Country Public Library, Centereach, New York. Photo credit: Middle Country Public Library.

childhood service. Materials to be used in the early childhood programs can be stored in closed cabinets or bins, out of sight when the room is used for other groups. If there is no separate meeting room, designate a quiet corner of the children's room for early childhood service.

Check the area for child safety—no sharp corners on furniture, no unstable furniture, no open stairways. Remove any breakable objects. Cover electrical outlets, and secure any electrical cords that cannot be placed out of reach.

Bookshelves should be open and low enough for toddlers to reach for books and choose for themselves. The shelves should be secured to the wall or heavy enough so that they cannot be pulled over. Whenever possible, display books face out.

Store learning toys and other program materials in boxes that can be locked. Special bookcases can be purchased for holding small board books. Racks designed for holding book and cassette kits are also available. Label materials and their storage locations so that children and their parents and caregivers can easily find and return them.

Accommodate toddlers' special physical needs with low chairs and tables. Provide a few comfortable chairs for lap reading, provide a parking place for strollers, and add a diaper changing table to the restroom facilities.

Carpeting reduces noise and offers children and parents and caregivers a comfortable place to sit while browsing or participating in programs. If carpeting is too expensive, consider a washable area rug that can be stored when not in use.

Children are known to respond positively to bright colors, but quiet tones are easier to live with over time. Liven up the area with child-appealing posters, such as clear pictures of friendly human faces and familiar animals. Add flowers and nonpoisonous plants.

If a separate room is available, you may want to organize the space into activity areas—for example:

1. make-believe (dramatic) play area with dress-up clothes, house-keeping equipment such as pots and pans, dolls with molded features and molded hair, and toy telephones and telephone books (homemade telephone books are easier for toddlers to handle)
2. block-bulding area with blocks, sorting and stacking toys, manipulative toys, and puzzles
3. music area with rhythm instruments (bells, drums, rhythm sticks), a record or cassette player, and recordings
4. arts and crafts area with clay, large paper, large crayons, paper towels, sponges, finger paints, tempera paints, construction paper, magic markers, and collage materials (This area should be near a sink. If no sink is available, eliminate finger painting and other activities that require washing up.)
5. reading-aloud and storytelling area with sturdy books of heavy paper or cardboard pages, low shelves with books facing out, pop-up books, and rockers or comfortable chairs for lap readings.

The floor plans of the Family Room at the New York Public Library's ECRIC (see fig. 19), the Children's Center at the Gail Borden Public Library in Elgin, Illinois (see fig. 20), the Parent/Child Workshop Room and the early childhood area at the Middle Country Public Library in Centereach, New York (see figs. 21 and 22) may suggest ideas for designing space in your library.

As for furnishings, librarians who have designed early childhood spaces have had to look outside the usual library furniture suppliers for appropriate storage cabinets, activity tables, seating, and shelving. Many have resorted to local carpenters and craftspeople, who have custom designed what is needed. (See vendor list on page 138.)

Unfortunately, there is little in the library literature to assist librarians in designing space for early childhood services. This is an area that deserves attention from the profession. Before designing the early childhood area at the Middle Country Public Library, Sandra Feinberg visited many child-center facilities, including the Gail Borden Public Library's Children's Center, the New York Public Library's ECRIC, the Boston Children's Museum,[5] day-care centers, FAO Schwarz toy store, and the children's furniture sections of department stores, to get ideas. Feinberg generously shared her in-house brochure *Designing Library Services for Early Childhood: Space and Environment* with the participants at the NYPL/NYU conference.[6]

In the education field, Lesley Mandel Morrow of Rutgers University School of Education has written extensively about environmental designs for the classroom.[7] Morrow views the physical setting as an active influence on classroom activities and recommends arranging the room in centers dedicated to particular activities or content areas, such as literacy, art, math, music, and so on. The literacy center, for example, includes the library corner, writing area, and oral language activities. Literacy is not limited to the literacy center, of course, but integrated into all the content areas. Many of Morrow's suggestions for designing classroom areas to promote literacy development can be applied to children's rooms in public libraries.

Publicity and Promotion

Word of mouth (librarian to parent, parent to parent, librarian to the staff of child-centered agencies in the community) is the best way to publicize the library's early childhood services. A list of target audiences and suggested contacts can be found in figure 23.

5. See Jeri Robinson, *Playspace: Creating Family Spaces in Public Places* (Boston: Boston Children's Museum, 1984).

6. Sandra Feinberg, *Designing Library Services for Early Childhood: Space and Environment* (Centereach, N.Y.: Middle Country Public Library, 1989). As this book goes to press, Feinberg and her staff are working on an expanded version of the brochure, which will be available for purchase from the Middle Country Public Library.

7. See, for example, Lesley Mandel Morrow, "Designing the Classroom to Promote Literacy Development," in *Emergent Literacy: Young Children Learn to Read and Write*, ed. Dorothy S. Strickland and Lesley Mandel Morrow (Newark, Del.: International Reading Association, 1989); and Lesley Mandel Morrow and C. S. Weinstein, "Increasing Children's Use of Literature through Programs and Physical Design Changes," *Elementary School Journal* 83 (1982) 131–37.

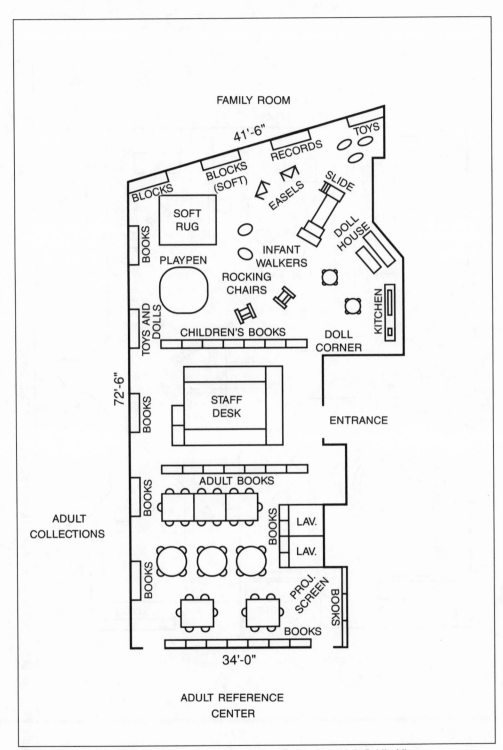

Figure 19. Early Childhood Resource and Information Center, New York Public Library

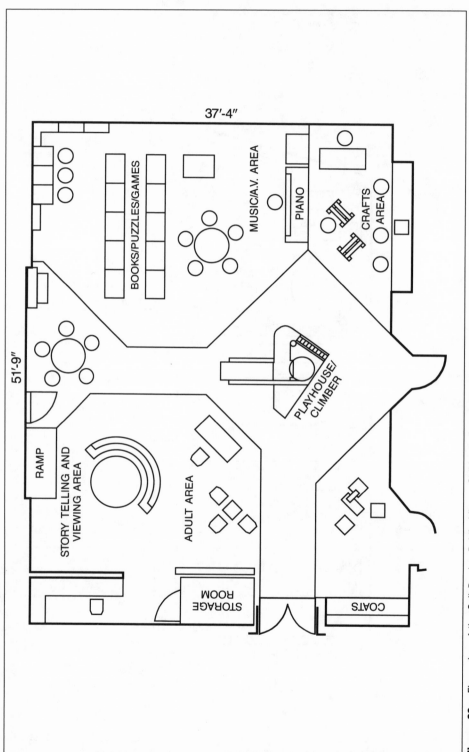

Figure 20. Floor plan of the Gail Borden Public Library Children's Center, Elgin, Illinois

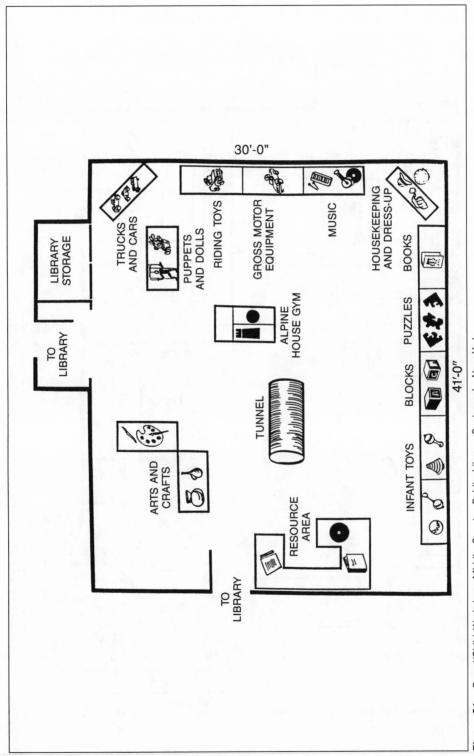

Figure 21. Parent/Child Workshop, Middle Country Public Library, Centereach, New York

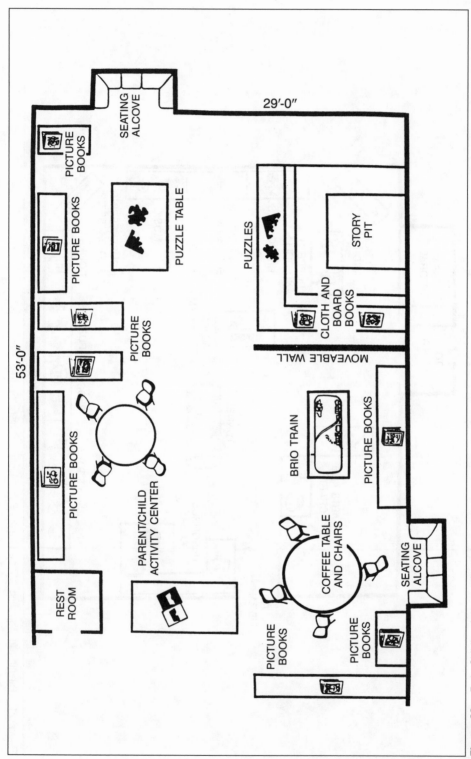

Figure 22. Early Childhood Area, Middle Country Public Library, Centereach, New York

Parents of Young Children; Expectant Parents
Contact: offices of pediatricians, obstetricians, child psychiatrists; La Leche Leagues; Lamaze classes; Mothers of Twins groups; Parents Without Partners groups; well baby clinics; child study associations; church and synagogue groups; local schools offering classes in family life; baby and children's departments in local stores.

Grandparents and Foster Grandparents
Contact: senior citizens' associations; retirement center recreation programs; foster grandparent programs; church and synagogue groups; municipal departments of aging.

Babysitters
Contact: local teen groups; high school classes in child care and family life; Red Cross chapters; 4-H clubs; scout groups; church and synagogue youth groups.

Playground and Playgroup Directors and Staffs
Contact: YMCAs; municipal recreation departments.

Religious Education Instructors
Contact: church and synagogue groups; retailers of religious goods; church-affiliated schools.

Preschool Teachers and Aides
Contact: preschools; Head Start programs; high schools, vocational schools, technical colleges and universities offering classes in child care or programs in early childhood education; local chapters of the Association for the Education of Young Children.

Child Care Center Staffs
Contact: child care centers; high schools, vocational schools, technical colleges, colleges and universities offering classes in child care or programs in early childhood education; local chapters of the Association for the Education of Young Children; community health nurses.

Family Caregivers
Contact: family caregiver associations; municipal and state licensing agents or agencies; community health nurses; food cooperatives (many have a newsletter); local chapters of the Association for the Education of Young Children; high schools, vocational schools, technical colleges, colleges and universities offering classes in child care or programs in early childhood education.

Pediatricians, Nurse Practitioners, Pediatric Residents, and Other Medical Professionals Who Work with Young Children
Contact: doctors' offices and clinics; well baby clinics; hospital programs for children (call the hospital's public relations department); medical schools (call the chief pediatrics resident).

Teachers and Students in Family Life, Child Care, Child Development, and Children's Literature Classes
Contact: high schools, vocational schools, technical colleges, colleges and universities.

Library Staffs
Contact: public libraries; school libraries; regional and state library associations and media organizations; library schools.

Figure 23.   Target audiences and suggested contacts, from "Programming, Planning, and Presentation," by Maralita L. Freeny in *First Steps to Literacy: Library Programs for Parents, Teachers, and Caregivers,* by Nell Colburn and Maralita L. Freeny (ALA, 1990), pp. 24–25.

Attractive flyers distributed in the library and in community places where parents gather—pediatric clinics, day-care centers, shelters, Laundromats, and so forth—will call attention to library programs. Keep the flyers simple, and be sure the information concerning date, time, place, and type of event is clearly stated.

There may be times when you wish to announce a special program in a more formal way. Local newspapers are usually willing to announce library programs. Know your newspaper's deadlines. Keep announcements brief but, as with the flyers, be sure to include all essential information—date, time, place, and topic (see fig. 24 for sample calendar listings). Public radio and television stations broadcast community bulletin board information. Call your local station manager regarding the proper procedure for submitting information.

Invite your newspaper to send a photographer and reporter to cover a large event, such as a family reading fair.

Plan tie-in's with national campaigns, such as the Week of the Young Child, National Library Week, and Children's Book Week.

Offer to write an article or prepare a parenting reading list for newsletters published by childcare agencies, housing projects, neighborhood

January 8, 15, 22, 29	10:30 a.m. "Mother Goose Storytime." A 4-week series of stories, songs, and activities, presented by Kathy McQuown for children 18 months to 3 years old, with accompanying adult. Registration is required; call (212) 548-5656, Kingsbridge Branch, 280 W. 231st St.
11, 18, 25	11:00 a.m. "Preschool Computer Workshop." An introduction to software appropriate for preschoolers using the Library's Apple Computer. For children ages 2 to 4, accompanied by an adult. Call (718) 351-1444 for preregistration. (Attendance at all three sessions is strongly recommended.) Supported by a special grant from the Carnegie Foundation. Dongan Hills Branch, 1617 Richmond Rd.
8, 15, 22	10:30 a.m. "Mother and Child Reunion." A 3-session class of lap baby songs and games for parents and their 6- to 12-month-old babies. There will be a variety of patting, bouncing, tickling, cuddling, and feeding games as well as lullabies and songs. Preregistration is required; call (212) 744-5284, Yorkville Branch, 222 E. 79th St.

Figure 24. Sample calendar listings from *Events for Children* (Branch Libraries, New York Public Library)

coalitions, schools, churches, and so on in your community. Include a brief description of library services in your article.

Figure 25 shows a sample flyer from the NOLA Regional Library System in Youngstown, Ohio, promoting a program available for booking. The information given is clear and concise.

TITLE: RAISING FUTURE READERS: SHARING BOOKS WITH BABIES, TODDLERS, AND PRESCHOOLERS

A PROGRAM FOR: THE YEAR OF THE YOUNG READER

WHO: ANY INTERESTED NOLA LIBRARY

PRESENTER: Sue McCleaf-Nespeca, Youth Services Consultant, NOLA

INTENDED AUDIENCE: PARENTS, EARLY CHILDHOOD TEACHERS, CAREGIVERS OF YOUNG CHILDREN

PROGRAM: LECTURE FORMAT. Introductory information presented, followed by the sharing of many books. A handout with book titles will be distributed.

LENGTH: 1 to 1¼ hours (includes time for browsing/questions) (can be shorter if presented at the same time as an existing program, such as preschool storytime)

WHEN: Since this is a program for adults, the programs will probably need to be scheduled in the evening.

WHAT YOU MUST DO: • Advertise program. (Contacts can be made with early childhood educators; flyers can be distributed in the library, doctors' offices, etc. Also, programs can be advertised in the paper.)

• Set up room or area. Lectern will be needed along with tables (2) to display books.

• Arrange refreshments if desired.

PLEASE NOTE: A limited number of engagements (approx. 2 a month) can be scheduled. Bookings will be accepted for late April, May, September, October, and November.

TO BOOK: RESERVATIONS ACCEPTED BEGINNING **MARCH 23.** PLEASE CALL THE NOLA OFFICE AT 746-7042 AND MAKE ARRANGEMENTS WITH SUE.

Figure 25. Sample promotion flyer

Many libraries have produced professional and attractive materials of interest to parents and caregivers, such as *Babies and Books: A Joyous Beginning* (Decatur Public Library, Illinois), *A Stitch in Time: Enhancing Your Baby's Development through Books and Language Activities* (Dauphin County Library System, Harrisburg, Pennsylvania), *Babies and Books: A Calendar for Babies and Parents* (Prince George Public Library, British Columbia), and *Growing to Love Books* (New York Public Library).[8]

The Las Vegas–Clarke County Library District designed a special card for children younger than age six. Called "My First Library Card" and printed in bright yellow, it depicts a green parent turtle with five little green turtles (see fig. 26).

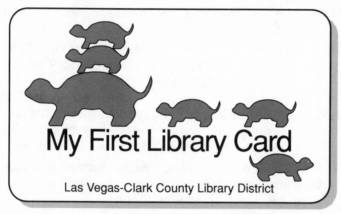

Figure 26. Sample library card for young children

Evaluation

Evaluation is important and necessary to any area of library service. Even seemingly successful programs must be assessed as to their value to users and to the library planners.

The purpose of evaluation is to assess the degree of success in achieving short- and long-range goals and objectives. Therefore, the evaluation process should be developed during the planning stage, when you are defining your goals and objectives. How will you know you have accomplished what you set out to do? A sample evaluation tool for specific objectives can be found as figure 27.

8. Claudia Quigg and Katie Gross, *Babies and Books: A Joyous Beginning*, a Baby Talk Publication, illus. Tomie de Paola (Decatur, Ill.: Decatur Public Library, 1988); Sara J. Willoughby-Herb and Steven L. Herb, *A Stitch in Time: Enhancing Your Baby's Development through Books and Language Activities* (Harrisburg, Pa.: Dauphin County Library System, 1984); Barb Dean and Joan Jarman, *Babies and Books: A Calendar for Babies and Parents* (Prince George, B.C.: Prince George Public Library, 1986); Ellin Greene, *Growing to Love Books*, illus. Shirley Hughes and Jan Ormerod (New York: New York Public Library, 1989). This growth chart was funded by a grant from the Carnegie Corporation of New York in connection with the New York Public Library's Early Childhood Project.

Evaluation Tool

Identify the objective:

Was it achieved? _____ Yes   _____ No   _____ Partially

If the answer is no or partially:

1. Was lack of time a factor?
   Possible solution:

2. To what extent was the target population reached quantitatively?
   (This may be measured by survey, questionnaire, or active count of
   users.)

   Possible methods to increase numbers, if desired:

3. What resources were lacking?
   Possible solution:

4. How was the population affected?
   Desired effect:

   Actual effect:

   Possible solution:

Repeat for each objective.

Figure 27. Sample evaluation form for staff use

Be prepared to document the service. Documentation can be formal or
informal. Formal documentation includes circulation and attendance
records, statistical charts, responses to surveys, and other such information.
It should also include such measurables as preparation time in proportion
to staff performance, and cost effectiveness of publicity generated in relation
to actual program time. Informal documentation includes anecdotal evidence, letters and testimonials from the public (see fig. 29), and evidence of
interest generated among the public and press.

Figure 28. A sampling of materials of interest to parents and caregivers

The most familiar evaluation tool is the questionnaire submitted to a program's participants. A sample questionnaire used to evaluate a parent-child literature-sharing program is figure 30.

I am writing to thank you for the recent four-week toddler program at the Bloomingdale Branch of the library. My daughter, Kathryn, who is almost three, and I were very sorry to see it end and we hope that it will be possible for the program to run again....It was obvious that much time and thought had been put into planning the program and more specifically, a theme for each week's books....

Often, the suburbs are touted to committed city dwellers for the availability of more personalized services to children at libraries, etc. It is programs like this one that are so helpful to parents of youngsters. Beyond developing an appreciation for books and the Library and all it has to offer, it gave us an opportunity to make some new friends and enjoy the fellowship of our urban peers.

Figure 29. A letter received by the New York Public Library's Manhattan Borough Office from a pleased patron.

Evaluation Form for Parent-Child Literature-sharing Program

Name _____

Address _____

Child's name _____

Child's age _____ Birthdate _____

Today's date _____

1. Where did you first find out about the parent-child program?

_____ newspaper   _____ library flyer or poster

_____ neighbor/friend   _____ other (please specify)_____

2. Were the day and time of the program convenient?

_____ yes   _____ no

If no, what would have been a better day and time?

_____ morning _____ early afternoon _____ evening

_____ Saturday _____ another weekday (please specify) _____

3. How appropriate were the materials used for the children?

	very appropriate	somewhat appropriate	inappropriate
a. stories			
b. music			
c. fingerplays			
d. film or video			

4. Would you be interested in a list of the books and the words of the songs and fingerplays used in the program?

_____ yes   _____ no

5. How often did you repeat some elements of the program at home?

	often	sometimes	never
a. stories			
b. songs			
c. fingerplays			

6. Have you noticed any change in your child's interest in books and stories since attending the program?

_____ no change _____ less interested _____ more interested

Figure 30. Sample evaluation form to give to participants

7. Did you have a library card before registering for the program? _____ yes   _____ no

8. As a result of this program, do you plan to use the library on a continuing basis? _____ yes   _____ no

9. Did you check out any library materials while you were in the library? _____ yes   _____ no

10. Would you be interested in a lecture series on parenting topics, such as nutrition, discipline or reading?
   _____ yes   _____ no

   If yes, please list the topics you would be interested in:

11. Would you recommend this program to other parents who have young children? _____ yes   _____ no

12. As a result of attending this program, do you spend more time

   a. playing with your child? _____ yes   _____ no

   b. talking with your child? _____ yes   _____ no

   c. reading with your child? _____ yes   _____ no

   d. listening to music or
      singing with your child? _____ yes   _____ no

13. What did you like best about the program?

14. What did you like least about the program?

15. Do you have any general comments or suggestions?

Thank you for taking time to complete this questionnaire. Your replies will help us plan other programs of interest to you and your child.

Figure 30. (continued)

Measuring the Unmeasurable

Our technological society demands measurable results, but for most children's librarians, it is the intangibles that make the commitment to early childhood service worthwhile. What does early childhood service mean to the librarian? To the user? I invited Denise Donavin, the mother of two boys who used the Gail Borden Public Library's Children Center, and Jill Bradish, a former staff member of the center who is now teaching in a Montessori school in New York state, to look back on the Children's Center. Donavin wrote:

> When I think of the preschool section of the public library in Elgin, I am flooded with memories...of my first son as an infant, crawling about, meeting books, blocks and puzzles, gerbils and goldfish...of building cardboard castles out of huge boxes on the library's back lawn during a Friday evening family program...of Dan's proud face when we received an award as the city's best readers...and just watching both of my boys grow to love a library as a very special place.
>
> Memories weren't quite enough, I thought, to write this piece, so I packed the kids into the car to visit a library we sadly left behind when we moved two years ago. As we approached the building, my four-year-old Craig saw the telltale bubble window and he remembered the place instantly. "The slide," he recalled, "Can I go on the slide?" But the first thing that caught his eye was a video of *Corduroy* and he sat down with other kids and their parents to watch the little bear's adventures. The video was a new addition to the parents' corner. Craig went on to meet a turtle puppet, then to climb the steps of the slide. The climber/slide may be the physical focal point of the room, but it isn't always the busiest spot. Kids soon learn that the puzzles, tapes, toys, crafts, costumes, and books are even more fun.
>
> In an hour, Craig gave a kangaroo puppet show; made a leaf rubbing; dialed our phone number in a miniature phone booth complete with a tot-sized authentic-looking pay phone; met a lizard, gerbil, hamster, and some goldfish (all safely ensconced in bubble-windowed cages and tanks); set a table for supper and served up plastic chicken and potatoes; watched "Corduroy"; demonstrated a marble game to a novice; and listened to a few stories—one was read by me, two were heard by eavesdropping on other parents (a common practice).
>
> This is a place moms and dads come on a Sunday, just to play and watch and share the fun. Parents learn a lot seeing their children in action. For example, my son Dan met Duplo blocks (preschool-sized Legos) at the library when he was about eighteen months old. It was the "wild man's" first sustained play ever. Concentrating on those Duplo blocks with such ferocity actually made him sit still. I immediately went out and bought some Duplos. At age eight, he's still building—with wood and nails—as well as with more complex Legos. When I told my sons it was time to leave, Craig said, "Only if we come again soon." Usually, departure is the only time of contention in this lively, peaceful library that kids don't want to leave. One of the saddest faces I ever saw in this room was on a little girl whose mother had waited until her

Shutting out a wintry day with a good book. Bubble window, Children's Center, Gail Borden Public Library. Photo credit: Cliff E. Lohs.

daughter was about to enter first grade before introducing her to the library. The librarian explained that she was too old for the preschool room, but now she could use the Youth Room. (Of course, the librarian let her stay and play awhile in the Children's Center.)

A banner in the Children's Center reads "Play is children's work." Play is their fun, their education, and their socialization as well. Play in the Children's Center leads to books—almost no one leaves without an armful of selections. But it leads even further—to the feeling that a library is a splendid place in which to spend some time."

Donavin's sentiments are echoed by Jill Bradish, former staff member:

I was hired for the Children's Center primarily because of my early childhood background. My B.S. degree is in preschool and primary education. I had previous experience as a school librarian and had taught nursery school and kindergarten. Some experience with preschoolers and their adult caregivers is a real plus in this work.

Our intent was to provide materials, ideas, and space for young children and their parents to play together, learn together, and read together. The staff planned, prepared, and oversaw the activities. It was the parents who carried them out. They were required to remain with their children, and the activities were designed to encourage parent participation.

Staff members were on hand to provide suggestions for appropriate age-level materials, advise on book selection, and conduct traditional library programs for children, parents, and teachers. Toddler storytimes were offered at various times throughout the week to accommodate different family schedules. We prepared extensive subject booklists and kept an up-to-date annotated notebook of available toys. A file of area preschools and childcare facilities was very popular with parents.

We got to know many of our families. Some came several times a week; others came only for programs. Evening and Saturday hours brought in lots of dads. Whole families would come on Sunday afternoons.

Once a year, we gave a workshop for teachers of preschoolers—sometimes the workshop was led by a member of the staff, sometimes by an outside resource person. The workshops were always well attended.

Programs for parents were not as successful. I don't think this was due to lack of interest, but rather to the fact that many other community agencies were addressing these needs. In communities where this is not true, I think it's important to offer programs for parents. Child development topics are an obvious choice, but it's also important to include a tour of the library and to show parents the full range of materials and services available to them.

Young children are a wonderful clientele to serve. They are curious, open to new experiences, and honest in their responses. Their parents are an equally stimulating group to serve. Most of them are truly interested in providing the best for their children. For librarians, the reward is seeing the parent and child sharing and enjoying a program we've developed for them; seeing them week after week as they become regular library users and life-long library supporters.

Appendix
Directory of Vendors

The following sources provided furnishings for Middle Country Public Library, Centereach, New York.

Childcraft
20 Kilmer Road
Edison, NJ 08818
Puppet theater

Child's Play
13 Mill Creek Road
Port Jefferson, NY 11777
Brio train board, puppets, puzzles

Document Management Group
    Library Bureau
30 Versey Street
New York, NY 10007
Display case—6-foot sliding glass door, oak benches with fabric

FAO Schwarz
P.O. Box 18225
Chattanooga, TN 37422
Large stuffed animals, red display case

Highsmith Co., Inc.
W5527 Highway 106
P.O. Box 800
Fort Atkinson, WI 53538-0800
Oak display cases—archives

Listening Library
One Park Avenue
Old Greenwich, CT 06870
Storybook characters

Marek Woodworking
247 Blue Point Avenue
Blue Point, NY 11715
Boat (book barge)

Tide-Rider
85 Corporate Drive
P.O. Box 12427
Hauppague, NY 11788
Large wood doll house

White Flower Farm
Route 63
Litchfield, CT 06759
Large oak bench

Workbench
2075 Smithhaven Plaza
Lake Grove, NY 11755
Children's oak tables and chairs

The following sources provided furnishings for Children's Center, Gail Borden Public Library, Elgin, Illinois.

Kids and Things Demco
Box 7488
Madison, WI 53707
Chairs

Worden Co.
Nordika Library Group
Holland, MI 49422
Shelves, desk, and tables

appendix

A

EARLY CHILDHOOD CENTERS: THREE MODELS

By Ellin Greene

Within the last twenty years, public library service to preschool children, parents, and professional child caregivers has expanded to a remarkable degree. The research and writings of Benjamin Bloom[1] of the University of Chicago and Burton White,[2] director of the Preschool Project at Harvard University, which emphasized the importance of the early years in learning and the parent as the child's first teacher, and the civil rights movement which demanded compensatory educational programs for children of economically poor blacks, brought about a change in attitude toward early childhood programs.

With the initiation of federally funded Head Start programs in 1965, children's librarians found their expertise in children's literature and storytelling in high demand by staff of these programs. They also found that the preschoolers in these programs were not used to being read to, and that simpler books, such as Munari's *Jimmy Has Lost His Cap* (World Publishing, 1954), were needed to hold their attention. In time, publishers began publishing more books for toddlers who were not ready for longer, more literary stories.

By the 1970s the traditional library preschool storytime for 3- to 5-year-olds (developed in the '30s) had been extended to younger children (18 months to 3 years old) through toddler hours and services to new parents. The highly successful "Catch 'em in the Cradle" and "Sharing Literature with Children"[3] programs started by the Orlando (Florida) Public Library are such programs. A recent survey conducted by Ann Carlson, as part of her doctoral study at Columbia University School of Library Service, indicated

SLJ 30:6 (February 1984): 21–27. Reprinted by permission of *School Library Journal*.

1. Bloom, Benjamin, ed. *Taxonomy of Educational Objectives*. David McKay, 1956.
2. White, Burton. *Experience and Environment: Major Influences on the Development of the Young Child*. Prentice-Hall, 1973.
3. Peterson, Carol Sue. "Sharing Literature with Children." In *Start Early for an Early Start*, ed. Ferne Johnson. ALA, 1976. p. 100–04.

that public libraries in 45 of the 50 states offer some form of literature-sharing programs for children under the age of three.[4]

The quintessence of public library service to the young child is the center specifically designed to meet the needs and interests of preschoolers and their caregivers. Five such centers were identified in the literature[5][6][7] or in the files of the Preschool Services and Parent Education Committee of the Association for Library Service to Children (ALSC) of the American Library Association. All five centers opened between 1972 and 1978. They are (1) the Media Library for Preschoolers of the Erie Public Library, Erie, Pennsylvania; (2) the Preschool Adventure Library of the Cambria County Library System, Johnstown, Pennsylvania; (3) the Center for Discovery of the Public Library of Columbus and Franklin County, Columbus, Ohio; (4) the Gail Borden Public Library Children's Center, Elgin, Illinois; and (5) the New York Public Library's Early Childhood Resource and Information Center in New York City.

Interest in these centers led to a comparative study, the subject of this paper. The purpose of the study was to find out the current status of the centers, and to compare them in regard to the following aspects: (1) origin and purpose; (2) scope of the collections and types of services; (3) ways in which this innovative service differs from traditional services to preschoolers. The study also aimed to identify (1) factors that contribute to the success or failure of a center; (2) factors to consider before starting a center; (3) competencies needed by a center's staff; (4) the implications of the need for such competencies for library education.

Methodology

A two-part questionnaire was sent to the director of each center, or, in the case of the now defunct Media Library for Preschoolers (MLP), to the present coordinator of children's services.

Part I of the questionnaire was open-ended, and attempted to elicit the director's or coordinator's attitude toward this type of library service, his or her perception of the goals and objectives of the center, and opinions on the kind of education that best prepares staff for working in an early-childhood center. Part II asked for descriptive and statistical data. Data for the defunct center were obtained from the present director of the Erie County Library System; files of this center were made available, and telephone interviews

4. Carlson, Ann. A Nationwide Survey of Librarians' Practices and Attitudes in Serving Children Under Three Years of Age and Their Parents and Caregivers. Doctoral dissertation, School of Library Service, Columbia University, 1983.

5. Shannon, Linda. "Preschool Adventure Library." *School Library Journal* 23, no. 3:25–27 (November 1975).

6. Sivulich, Kenneth G. and Sandra Sivulich. "Media Library for Preschoolers: A Service of the Erie Metropolitan Library." *Top of the News* 31, no. 1:49–54 (November 1974).

7. Savage, Noelle. "Special Report: N.Y.'s Early Childhood Center Serves Mothers and Caretakers." *Library Journal* 108, no. 1:13–14 (January 1983).

with the present coordinator of children's services and former staff members of the Media Library were held.

The questionnaire and telephone interviews were supplemented by visits to each of the three centers discussed. (Two of the centers turned out to be so specially oriented—the Preschool Adventure Library was a Montessori-based program and toy-lending library; the Center for Discovery is oriented to serve "disadvantaged preschool children and handicapped children who are chronically or developmentally pre-school-aged"—that it was decided not to include them.)

Profiles

The Media Library For Preschoolers (MLP) was the outcome of a study made by Kenneth G. Sivulich, then Director of the Erie Metropolitan Library, and Dale W. Craig, then Extension Librarian. The purpose of their study was to discover the public library needs of preschoolers in Erie. Based on the findings of the study it was decided that a *multimedia* center would best satisfy the needs of young users, since few were readers. In an interview published in *American Libraries*, Craig states that the MLP was designed "to introduce preschoolers to the library, to channel their curiosity with stimulating media experience, and to provide an alternative to structured preschool programs."[8]

The MLP, funded by a 2-year grant from the Library Services and Construction Act, was located on the first floor of a building formerly occupied by a local bank, six blocks south of the main library and easily accessible by public transportation. A facility was selected away from the main library because of lack of suitable space in that building. Theodore Pettersen, a media specialist and library administrator with an undergraduate degree in biological sciences and a graduate degree in pupil personnel services, was appointed director. Additional staff included a children's librarian, a media technician, supporting staff, and students in a work-study program who worked up to 15 hours a week.

When the MLP opened to the public on November 20, 1972, it was hailed as the prototype of public library services to young children. Public reaction was overwhelming. Within the first three months of operation over 1400 preschoolers registered for library cards and over 7200 items were borrowed by 2400 users. The average visit to the library lasted between one and 1½ hours. A majority (68%) of the children using the facility were between the ages of two and five, 12% were under age two, and 20% were ages five and six.

The writer's first impression of the MLP was of a large open space divided, not by walls, but by activity. A parent's lounge furnished with comfortable chairs, books and magazines on parenting, and disposable diapers and hot coffee were available. For the children there was a "Listening Cave"

8. Craig, Dale. "Preschool Library Service." *American Libraries* 4, no. 3:136 (March 1973).

with a built-in speaker for music, stories, etc.; a "whatever-you-want-it-to-be" platform, designed and built by a local architect; an animal corner with live animals—hamsters, gerbils, mice, rabbits, turtles, etc.; books, toys, audiovisual materials everywhere. A former bank vault had been converted into a story hour room; the vault door was kept open so that the children could see the tumblers, and the inside of the vault was decorated with Dr. Seuss and Sesame Street characters drawn on the walls by a local artist. Children and parents were playing together; some children were watching a filmstrip based on a children's book; others were listening to a story being read aloud, or playing with toys.

Ted Pettersen stressed the importance of the environment, one in which the child and his or her parents felt free to explore, "to wonder and discover." He considered the human element the most important in the program—openness, friendliness, patience, and a love of children. The key words, he stressed, were "spontaneity and awareness of preschoolers." Pettersen defended the center's innovative and controversial feature—the circulation of live animals—saying it gave children "insight into the mystery of life" and "encouraged responsibility."

He emphasized that the Media Library was not a babysitting service: an adult must be present, and he or she was free to participate in the many programs planned for parents. These included lectures, films, and craft activities. Lecture topics ranged from selecting toys to the effects of television on children. A Parent Handbook introduced parents to the services of the Media Library. The staff compiled many bibliographies, not only of books, but also of places to visit and things to do with young children in the Erie area. Volunteers, ranging in age from 12 to 65, worked under the guidance of a local volunteer agency. They read to children, taped and edited children's literature for the "Dial-a-Story" line, conducted story hours, and gave programs in the creative and performing arts. The Media Library offered a course, "Exploring Childhood," for 7th to 12th graders. This offered an opportunity for students to learn about child development and experience working with young children.

When I visited the Media Library for Preschoolers in 1974, project funds were ending and the center was to be relocated in the Main Library. An information sheet for the public stated: "The services of the Media Library will continue as part of the total services of the Children's Department of the Erie Metropolitan Library once the federal funding has expired. Since the response from the community has been so overwhelmingly favorable, it would be impossible to end the service completely." The staff expressed concern about the consequences of the move and their concerns were borne out when the Main Library was unable to assimilate the innovative service in its tradition-bound setting. Today, only fragments of the collections remain.

The Gail Borden Public Library's Children's Corner in Elgin, Illinois opened on January 13, 1978. The library already had a strong children's program, but two grants afforded funds for additional space and resources, as well as staff to develop an innovative service and creative programming for young children and their parents. The Local Public Works Act of 1976 provided a grant for the remodeling of the library's original meeting room (40'×52') and the addition of a sky-lighted atrium (24'×18'), thus creating the new Children's Center. A Library Services and Construction Act grant matched funds expended from the local library budget for a two-year period; this made possible an extensive expansion of the collection and the addition of one professional and one part-time clerk. The library matched this staffing.

When the federal funds expired, the library retained the Children's Center and its staff of two full-time professionals and two part-time clerks, evidence of its support and commitment to the program. The regular library budget does not allow for experimenting, but the Center's director, Mary Greenawalt, feels there is less need for experimentation at this point. Relying on experience and user response, buying priorities have been set; fewer toys are purchased and emphasis is given to those that are used in the library, have developmental value, and which may be too expensive for home purchase. Cassette/book kits and records, the most popular of the non-book media, make up the largest percentage of the audiovisual acquisitions. The Center has acquired audiovisual equipment and a piano.

The goal of the Children's Center is "to establish a life-time habit of library use." The director described the Children's Center as "an environment where parents and teachers can work with preschool children to create and support opportunities for intellectual and social growth...it is designed for adults and children communicating and interacting with each other."

The Center is located on the main floor of the library, diagonally across from the Youth Room, which serves children six years and older. When the Center first opened it served children from infants through age seven, but it soon became apparent to the staff that first and second graders are physically too big for the room and that their interests demand a wider range of books. Consequently, a major portion of their materials and activities was moved to the Youth Room. The Children's Center now concentrates on serving preschoolers and kindergarteners and their caregivers.

The Children's Center is an inviting area dominated by a playhouse/climber/slide, a favorite spot for the preschoolers but a controversial item among visiting librarians. Perhaps because most of the furniture is fixed rather than movable, the Children's Center has a neater, more orderly look than the Erie MLP. There is a pleasant hum, and the users—both adult and children—obviously feel very much at home. Like the Media Library for Preschoolers, the Children's Center is divided into activity areas for browsing among its 8000 books and over 1500 non-book items. The Parents' Corner contains a permanent collection of about fifty books on parenting which is supplemented with a rotating collection of 150 titles from the adult services department. Other materials in this section include magazines, pamphlets, and a resource file on health and recreational services for children available in the community, an annually updated booklet with information about area nursery schools and day care centers, and a weekly hand-out card of "Hints for Parents."

A survey made in 1979 showed a dramatic increase in the number of preschoolers and adults using the library (51% and 124% respectively), and in the circulation of books and non-book materials (30% and 100% respectively). A recent survey, taken five years after the Center opened, shows even greater gains—the Children's Center is thriving. The library board, administration, and staff are committed to the concept of a center for preschoolers and supportive of the wide variety of activities that encourage reading readiness and media awareness for preschoolers.

The Children's Center is viewed as an integral part of the library and its services. There is space to accommodate the sounds and movement that preschool activities generate. The staff have enthusiasm, stamina, and expertise to work with preschoolers. The director has an undergraduate degree in education and a graduate degree in library science. Her assistants have degrees in early childhood, education, or librarianship. The director remarked: "We have had the Children's Center for five years now, and the staff and the public take the facility somewhat for granted. I believe the Center is an important and vital community resource. At worst the Children's Center is a babysitting service for adults when they leave to select books in the adult department; at best it is a rich learning environment for caring parents and their preschool children. It serves a significant cross-section of the community, racially, culturally, and economically. We probably do not offer as many opportunities for parent education as originally planned, but I make no apology for this. We have come to realize our expertise is in the selection and use of children's media. We sponsor workshops and seminars in this area, and we serve the media needs of two colleges, two senior high schools, and a YWCA and a YMCA and other community agencies which offer courses for parents and childcare givers."

The Early Childhood Resource and Information Center (ECRIC) of the New York Public Library is located on the second floor of the Hudson Park Branch in west Greenwich Village. Its neighbors include New York University, the New School for Social Research and the Little Red School House. The community residents are politically active, highly educated, articulate, and are staunch supporters of the Center.

The Center is the brainchild of Barbara Rollock, Coordinator of Children's Services at the New York Public Library, and opened on October 26, 1978. Original funding came from a bequest by the poet and children's book author, Mary Agnes Miller. Mrs. Rollock wrote up the proposal as a one-year demonstration project. Support was so high by the end of the year, it would have been inconceivable for the library to close the Center.

Much of the credit goes to the director, Hannah Nuba Scheffler, a former staff member who has a master's degree in library science and is currently studying for a doctorate in early childhood from New York University; she was persuaded to return from early retirement to set it up. Mrs. Scheffler is assisted by a full-time professional, a half-time professional, a part-time clerk, and a part-time page. An advisory committee composed of 185 persons—educators, librarians, psychologists, health care providers, and parents—lends strong support. Approximately 35 members attend the bi-monthly meetings—a nucleus—plus those who come whenever they can (some live at a considerable distance from the city). Members do whatever needs to be done, from canvassing local politicians to giving workshops or writing articles.

Unlike the two centers described in which the emphasis is on parent-child interaction, the New York Public Library Early Childhood Resource and Information Center is oriented toward serving adults—"parents (single, teenage, grand, foster, prospective) as well as those who work in the fields of early childhood education, day care, Head Start, family day care, pre-kindergarten, and who are health professionals, babysitters, family-life educators, librarians, childcare workers, teachers, and social workers." Over 14,000 adults from all over the world visited the center in 1982.

ECRIC offers three major services: (1) a resource collection of over 6,000 books, pamphlets, periodicals, recordings, films and filmstrips on early childhood, and a browsing collection of over 4500 items for children. The focus is on materials "that promote the child's growth in a variety of ways, especially in language development and preliterary skills."

(2) A Family Room, an area that is arranged to encourage interaction between child and caregiver. This area includes a picture-book nook, a dramatic play space, music, art, science, and math corners, infant and toddler toys, playpens, infant walkers, rocking horses and rocking chairs, and a climber slide. The area is used as a place for parents and children to play together, or for children to play in while their parents attend a workshop or seminar presented at the other end of the room. The circulation desk separates the Family Room from the "library" where the resource collection is housed and the workshop/seminars take place. There are no dividing walls, so children in the Family Room are visible to the staff or parents at all times.

(3) An ongoing program of workshops and seminars that are conducted by educators and practitioners who contribute their time and expertise to the center. Four or five workshop/seminars are held each week. Recent programs included "The Language of Stories," by Dr. Jerome Bruner; "What Every Child Needs From His Parents," by Dr. Louise Ames; and "The Cultural and Political Context of Child Development: Fantasy and Reality," by Dr. Joseph Church. An annual conference in October presents an opportunity for elected officials, civic leaders, and the general public to get together to discuss issues and policies that affect the well-being of children. The center is in the process of developing video programs for home use and establishing a telephone "hot line" service for parents.

Recently the center published *Resources for Early Childhood: An Annotated Bibliography and Guide for Educators, Librarians, Health Care Professionals, and Parents*, edited by Hannah Nuba Scheffler, with contributions by members of the Advisory Committee (Garland, 1983).

Comparisons

The profiles of each center reveal many commonalities as well as significant differences. All three centers were established in urban areas. This suggests that only a fairly large system would have sufficient budget and staff to support a center. All three required a substantial initial financial outlay and received support from either a private bequest or federal funding.

The types of materials found in the centers are similar—books, recordings, films, filmstrips, puppets, puzzles, toys, multimedia kits, and learning games. The Early Childhood Resource and Information Center has the largest collection of materials for adult users and is more a "library" in the traditional sense.

Each center is or was a facility specifically designed to meet the needs of young children. The centers were developed as media libraries, based on the theories of Piaget, Montessori, and other developmental psychologists which stress that a child's first learning is sensory-motor oriented.

Two of the three centers are primarily oriented to parent-child interaction. One, the Early Childhood Resource and Information Center, is oriented toward parents and professional child care-givers, but has a Family Room designed for interaction between child and adult. This center is open on Saturdays, but not in the evenings, whereas the defunct Media Library for Preschoolers was open on Saturday and Sunday and weekday evenings for the convenience of working parents, as is the Children's Center.

The centers offer similar programs—story times, song and rhythmic activities for the children; parent-child programs, and workshop/seminars for adults (see table). The Media Library for Preschoolers emphasized informal adult-child interaction stimulated by the media environment. The Children's Center also emphasizes informal adult-child interactions, but in addition offers structured programs for toddlers. The Early Childhood Resource and Information Center has only recently initiated a structured program for toddlers. "Mommy, Daddy and Me at the Library" consists of stories "designed to foster emerging reading skills and language development" and related activities, such as dance movement, music, art, or dramatic play. ECRIC's strength lies in its collections and its workshops and seminars which offer parents and professional child caregivers an opportunity to interact with experts in the field and to keep up with the latest theories in developmental psychology. These programs are open to the public without charge.

All three centers share a similar philosophy of service to preschoolers and their caregivers. All consider this a part of *total* library service to the community. The Media Library for Preschoolers was the most innovative of the three, both in concept and physical arrangement; it was also the only center that was physically separated from its parent organization.

Observations

Formal evaluations were conducted by two of the three centers. These were highly positive. Even where there was no formal evaluation (as in the case of the Early Childhood Resources and Information Center), public response has been highly enthusiastic. The staff of all three centers rated this type of service superior to traditional library service to preschoolers. Why, then, have two of the centers flourished while the Media Library for Preschoolers has gone out of existence?

The failure of the Media Library for Preschoolers seems due to at least three factors, in addition to loss of funding: (1) relocation; (2) loss of original staff; (3) political considerations. When federal funding ended, the Media Library was moved into the main library where the lower level of the library was renovated to accommodate it on a smaller scale. The staff was kept intact for a year. At that time the city and county libraries decided to merge. The city library had been under the jurisdiction of the Board of Education. When the city and county libraries merged, the school district withdrew its financial support. The library director (who was also the co-creator and vital force behind the Media Library for Preschoolers) found his energy and time was absorbed by the political situation and diverted from the Media Library. When both the library director and the director of the Media Library left the system, the center just faded away. Lack of suitable space in the main library building, loss of the original staff, and less staff, severely limited the program. The overall community felt no necessity for the program, but individual users still remember the service favorably and still request that it be reinstated. Mothers report that their children who used the Media Library are "different" from their other children—they enjoy reading more, read more, and use the library more frequently. Since the names of the children who registered at the Media Library are on file it would be possible—and interesting—to do a follow-up study.

The necessary ingredients for success of a center seem to be: (1) a library board, administration, and a staff committed to, and supportive of, the concept of a media center offering preschoolers a wide variety of activities that encourage reading readiness. The center is integral to the library's services, not an "extra."

(2) Ample funding over a long enough period of time to establish the service in the public eye. Respondents to the questionnaire cautioned against starting a center without assurance of funding at the end of the grant period. The director of the Children's Center pointed out that once the program is established it is not any more expensive than special services offered to other identifiable library groups.

(3) A physical facility separate from but in proximity to the youth services area; space that can accommodate the sounds and movement that preschool activities generate—a multimedia environment designed to meet the sensory-motor orientation of young children.

(4) Staff which has the patience, stamina, enthusiasm, and expertise to serve preschoolers and their caregivers. This type of service requires expertise in librarianship and in early childhood education. Continuity of staff helps too.

(5) High public awareness and appreciation of the center's services— success comes through public awareness and support. The two existing centers had advisory committees which lent strong support while the centers were getting started.

When asked what are the most important factors to consider before starting a center for preschoolers, the respondents emphasized (1) community need, (2) adequate funding, and (3) qualified staff. Obviously, it is important to assess the needs of the community, to coordinate existing services for young children and their caregivers, and to be assured of adequate funding, before expanding service. Equally important, and sometimes overlooked, is the need for qualified personnel. The best educational background for staff working in a public library for preschoolers, according to all respondents, is early childhood education. Next is experience in library service with an emphasis on programming. Other disciplines checked as important were education, psychology, music, and art. Two respondents emphasized the importance of administrative ability. Staff are expected to be competent in materials evaluation (book and non-book), programming, ability to work with young children, parents, and professionals in the childcare fields. Patience, stamina, and a liking for children are basic. All respondents recommended that universities offer a joint degree in librarianship and early childhood. All noted the necessity of courses in child development, programming, administration and management, as well as courses in library materials and services to young children. This response supports the literature which substantiates the need for more adequate preparation for librarians who work with young children.[9] Yet only a few of the 69 accredited library schools in the United States and Canada, judging from their current announcements, offer courses specifically designed for service to young children and their caregivers.

Research indicates that parents expect public libraries to provide service to young children,[10][11] that early childhood educators support the concept,[12] and that there is a relationship between early language experiences, adult-child interaction, play activities, and reading aloud, to the child's interest in reading and use of the public library.[13][14][15][16] The Media Library for Preschoolers may have been too ambitious, but it provided the prototype for future library service to preschoolers.

An increase in the number of young children in the population is projected for 1990. A rising birth rate, especially among older, better-

9. Smardo, Frances A. "Are Librarians Prepared to Serve Young Children?" *Journal of Education for Librarianship* 20, no. 4:274–84 (Spring 1980).

10. Fasick, Adele. "Parents and Teachers View Library Service to Children." *Top of the News* 35, no. 3:309–14 (Spring 1979).

11. Young, Diana. "Parents—Children—Libraries." *PLA Newsletter* 16 no. 4:16–18 (Winter 1977).

12. Smardo, Frances A. An Analytical Study of the Recommendations of Early Childhood Education Authorities with Regard to the Role of the Public Library in Serving Children from Infancy to Six Years of Age. ERIC Document ED160 222, 1978.

13. Clarke, Margaret M. *Young Affluent Readers*. Heinemann Educational Books, 1976.

14. Clarke-Stewart, K.A., and N. Apfel. "Evaluating Parental Effects on Child Development." In *Review of Research in Education*, ed. Lee Shulman, vol. 6. F.E. Peacock, 1979.

15. Johnson, Ferne O. "Library Services Benefit Preschoolers." *Catholic Library World* 50 no. 5:212–17 (December 1978).

16. Teale, W. "Positive Environments for Learning to Read: What Studies of Early Readers Tell Us." *Language Arts* 55 no. 8:922–32 (November/December 1978).

educated parents who are more aware of the importance of the early years in learning, is likely to create increasing demands for high-quality library service to preschoolers. The centers now in operation demonstrate that the public library can offer a supportive but neutral learning environment for young children and their caregivers. Communities planning to construct a new library facility or to engage in a renovation (LSCA Title II funds are once again available after a moratorium of ten years) may want seriously to consider opening a Center to provide this innovative and exciting new development in library service.

appendix

B

EARLY CHILDHOOD: LIBRARY MATERIALS AND SERVICES

Early Childhood: Library Materials and Services is a graduate-level course designed for professional librarians employed by the New York Public Library who are working, or expect to work, with young children and their parents and caregivers. Upon completion of the course, three academic credits will be awarded to the student by New York University.

Goals and Objectives

1. To familiarize the student with current research in early childhood and its implications for library service to very young children and their parents and caregivers.
2. To familiarize the student with the history of library service to early childhood and various models of service, with emphasis on the ECRIC model.
3. To familiarize the student with the developmental characteristics of children from birth through age 3.
4. To familiarize the student with print and nonprint materials appropriate for very young children and their parents and caregivers, criteria for selecting such materials, and guidelines for their use.
5. To develop the student's expertise in storytelling, reading aloud, and other strategies for nurturing early interaction with stories and print.
6. To familiarize the student with socioeconomic conditions, ethnicity, family culture, etc. that affect library service to early childhood.
7. To develop the student's expertise in interacting with parents and community agencies.
8. To develop the student's expertise in administering library service to early childhood, planning and publicity, staff training, recruiting and training volunteers, etc.
9. To assist the student in designing and implementing a model program in early childhood for the branch library community in which the student works.

150

Methodology

The course will contain lecture, group discussion, readings, audiovisual presentations, observation of model programs, hands-on activities, etc.

Syllabus

1. Overview of the course. Goals and objectives, methodology, and requirements. Historical development and present status of library service to young chldren and their caregivers. Model library programs, with emphasis on the New York Public Library's Early Childhood Resource and Information Center. Contemporary theories of child development and early learning—Erikson, Montessori, Piaget, White, and their implications for library collections and services for early childhood.
2. Developmental characteristics of children from birth through age 3. Film: "Summary Program" (56 minutes), edited by Burton L. White—overview of the entire learning process from birth to the third birthday. Discussion of film and its implications for library service to children under age 3 and their caregivers.
3. Language development. Early literacy. Film: "The Foundations of Reading and Writing" (40 minutes).
4. Books for babies and toddlers. Types of materials available (Mother Goose and nursery rhymes, ABCs and counting books, concept books, traditional literature, modern imaginative stories, realistic stories, wordless books, toy books, etc.). Criteria for selection for the library collection. Helping parents select materials for their children.
5. Nonprint materials for young children (films, filmstrips, recordings, educational games and toys, computer software). Criteria for selection for the library collection. Guidelines for parents.
6. Designing a model program in early childhood service for your library community. Assessing your community's needs in early childhood. Planning, implementing, and evaluating library service to early childhood. Assessing published research in early childhood.
7. Literature-sharing programs for early childhood. Storytelling and reading aloud. The child's concept of story and the importance of story in child development. Film: "The Power of Stories" (17 minutes). Techniques of sharing literature with young children. Parent-child interaction. Infant programs and toddler hours.
8. Library materials and services for 4 and 5-year-olds. Picture book hours. Film programs. Planning, implementing, and evaluating library programs for this age group.
9. Observation of an early childhood literature-sharing program, followed by class discussion. Planning, implementing, and evaluating literature-sharing programs.

10. Outreach service—working with community groups. Coordinating and integrating community service to early childhood. Recruiting and utilizing volunteers in the library's program.
11. Parent education. Understanding and working with parents of young children. Influence of socioeconomic conditions, ethnicity, family culture, and television on child development, acquisition of language, reading readiness, and the use of library services. Parenting skills. Helping parents interact with their children. Resources for parents and other caregivers.
12. Serving young children with special needs (gifted, handicapped, bilingual).
13. Administering library service to early childhood. Implementing and maintaining optimum learning environments for early childhood. Child advocacy. Networking. Staff training.
14. Student reports on their model projects.
15. Student reports on their model projects (continued). Summary and evaluation of the course.

Background Reading for Professionals

Books

Anderson, Richard C., et al. *Becoming a Nation of Readers: The Report of the Commission on Reading.* Champaign, Ill.: Center for the Study of Reading, 1985.

Association for Library Service to Children, Preschool Services and Parent Education Committee. *First Steps to Literacy: Library Programs for Parents, Teachers, and Caregivers.* Chicago: American Library Association, 1990.

Baechtold, Marguerite, and Eleanor Ruth McKinney. *Library Service to Families.* Hamden, Conn.: Shoe String/Library Professional Publications, 1983.

Baghban, Marcia. *Our Daughter Learns to Read and Write: A Case Study from Birth to Three.* Newark, Del.: International Reading Association, 1984.

Baker, Augusta, and Ellin Greene. "Storytelling to Infants and Toddlers." In *Storytelling: Art and Technique.* 2nd ed. New York: Bowker, 1987.

Beck, M. Susan. *KIDSPEAK: How Children Develop Language Skills.* New York: Plume, 1982.

Bissex, Glenda. *GNYS AT WRK: A Child Learns to Write and Read.* Boston: Harvard University Press, 1980.

Bloom, Benjamin. *Stability and Change in Human Characteristics.* New York: Wiley, 1964.

Britton, James. *Language and Learning.* London: Penguin, 1970.

Brooks, Ellen J. *Learning to Read and Write: The Role of Language Acquisition and Aesthetic Development.* New York: Garland, 1986.

Butler, Dorothy. *Babies Need Books*. 2nd ed. New York: Penguin, 1988.

———. *Cushla and Her Books*. Boston: Horn Book, 1980.

———, and Marie Clay. *Reading Begins at Home: Preparing Children for Reading before They Go to School*. American edition prepared with the assistance of Bobbye S. Goldstein. Portsmouth, N.H.: Heinemann, 1987.

Cambourne, Brian. "Language, Learning and Literacy." In *Towards a Reading-Writing Classroom*. Edited by Andrea Butler and Jan Turbill. Portsmouth, N.H.: Heinemann, 1987.

Carlson, Ann D. *Early Childhood Literature Sharing Programs in Libraries*. Hamden, Conn.: Shoe String/Library Professional Publications, 1985.

Cazden, Courtney, ed. *Language in Early Childhood Education*. Rev. ed. Washington, D.C.: National Association for the Education of Young Children, 1981.

Chukovsky, Kornei. *From Two to Five*. Rev. ed. Translated and edited by Miriam Morton. Berkeley: University of California Press, 1968.

Clark, Margaret M. "Literacy at Home and at School: Insights from a Study of Young Fluent Readers." In *Awakening to Literacy*, edited by Hillel Goelman, Antoinette Oberg, and Frank Smith. Portsmouth, N.H.: Heinemann, 1984.

Cochran-Smith, Marilyn. *The Making of a Reader*. Norwood, N.J.: Ablex, 1984.

Crago, Maureen, and Hugh Crago. *Prelude to Literacy: A Preschool Child's Encounter with Picture and Story*. Carbondale: Southern Illinois University Press, 1983.

Cullinan, Bernice E. *Literature and the Child*. 2nd ed. San Diego: Harcourt Brace Jovanovich, 1989.

De Salvo, Nancy, Faith Hektoen, and Frank Self. *Resource List for Adults of Materials to Use with the Very Young Child*. Farmington, Conn.: Farmington Library, 1982.

De Villiers, Peter A. and Jill G. De Villiers. *Early Language*. Cambridge, Mass.: Harvard University Press, 1979.

Doake, David B. "Reading-like Behavior: Its Role in Learning to Read." In *Observing the Language Learner*, edited by Angela M. Jaggar and M. Trika Smith-Burke. Newark, Del.: International Reading Assoc. 1985.

Doman, Glenn. *How to Teach Your Baby How to Read*. Rev. ed. Philadelphia: Better Baby, 1983.

Durkin, Delores. *Children Who Read Early: Two Longitudinal Studies*. New York: Teachers College Press, 1966.

Elkind, David. *Miseducation: Preschoolers at Risk*. New York: Knopf, 1987.

———, and Irving B. Weiner. *Development of the Child*. New York: Wiley, 1978.

Erikson, Erik H. *Childhood and Society*. 2nd rev. ed. New York: Norton, 1964.

Feinberg, Sandra, and Kathleen Deere. *The Parent/Child Workshop: A Program Handbook*. New York: Suffolk Cooperative Library System, 1985.

Fraiberg, Selma H. *The Magic Years: Understanding and Handling Problems of Early Childhood*. New York: Scribner, 1959, 1984.

Gardner, Howard. *Artful Scribbles: The Significance of Children's Drawings*. New York: Basic Books, 1980.

Gettman, David. *Basic Montessori: Learning Activities for Under-Fives*. New York: St. Martin's Press, 1987.

Glazer, Susan M. *Getting Ready to Read: Creating Readers from Birth through Six*. Englewood Cliffs, N.J.: Prentice-Hall, 1980.

Goelman, Hillel, Antoinette Oberg, and Frank Smith. *Awakening to Literacy*. Portsmouth, N.H.: Heinemann, 1984.

Greenspan, Stanley and Nancy Thorndike Greenspan. *First Feelings: Milestones in the Emotional Development of Your Baby*. New York: Penguin, 1989.

Heath, Shirley Brice. *Ways with Words: Language, Life, and Work in Communities and Classrooms*. London: Cambridge University Press, 1983.

Holdaway, Don. *The Foundations of Literacy*. Portsmouth, N.H.: Heinemann, 1979.

Holt, John. *Learning All the Time: How Small Children Begin to Read, Write, Count, and Investigate the World without Being Taught*. Reading, Mass.: Addison-Wesley, 1989.

Hunt, J. McVicker. *Intelligence and Experience*. New York: Ronald Press, 1961.

Jaggar, Angela M., and M. Trika Smith-Burke. *Observing the Language Learner*. Newark, Del.: International Reading Association, 1985.

Kulleseid, Eleanor R., and Dorothy S. Strickland. *Literature, Literacy, and Learning: Classroom Teachers, Library Media Specialists, and the Literature-Based Curriculum*. Chicago: American Library Association, 1989.

Macchiarola, Frank K., and Alan Gartner, eds. *Caring for America's Children*. New York: Academy of Political Science, 1989.

McCracken, Robert A., and Marlene J. McCracken. *Stories, Songs, and Poetry to Teach Reading and Writing: Literacy through Language*. Chicago: American Library Association, 1986.

McLane, Joan Brooks, and Gillian Dowley McNamee. *Early Literacy*. Cambridge, Mass.: Harvard University Press, 1990.

McLaughlin, Barry. *Second Language Acquisition in Childhood*. Hillsdale, N.J.: Wiley, 1978.

Maier, Henry W. *Three Theories of Erik H. Erikson, Jean Piaget, and Robert R. Sears and Their Applications*. New York: Harper, 1965.

Meek, Margaret. *Learning to Read*. Portsmouth, N.J.: Heinemann, 1986.

Morrison, George S. *Education and Development of Infants, Toddlers, and Preschoolers*. Glenview, Ill.: Scott, Foresman, 1988.

Myers, Garry C., and Clarence W. Sumner. *Books and Babies*. Chicago: McClurg, 1938.

Nichols, Judy. *Storytimes for Two-Year-Olds*. Chicago: American Library Association, 1987.

Nuba Scheffler, Hannah, ed. *Infants: A Guide to Research and Resources*. New York: Garland, 1986. (A new edition is forthcoming.)

Paley, Vivian Gussin. *Molly Is Three: Growing Up in School*. Chicago: University of Chicago Press, 1986.

Papert, Seymour. *Mindstorms: Children, Computers, and Powerful Ideas*. New York: Basic Books, 1982.

Parker, Robert P., and Frances A. Davis, eds. *Developing Literacy: Young Children's Use of Language*. Newark, Del.: International Reading Association, 1983.

Piaget, Jean. *The Language and Thought of the Child*. New York: Harcourt, 1926.

Pulaski, Mary Ann. *Understanding Piaget*. Rev. ed. New York: Harper, 1980.

Roemer, Joan, as told to Barbara Austin. *Two to Four from 9 to 5: The Adventures of a Daycare Provider*. New York: Harper, 1989.

Rollock, Barbara T. "Early Childhood, Preschool, and Parent Education Programs." In *Public Library Services for Children*. Hamden, Conn.: Shoe String/Library Professional Publications, 1988.

Scheffler, Hannah, ed. *Resources for Early Childhood: An Annotated Bibliography and Guide for Educators, Librarians, Health Care Professionals, and Parents*. New York: Garland, 1983.

Schickedanz, Judith A. *More Than the ABCs: The Early Stages of Reading and Writing*. Washington, D.C.: National Association for the Education of Young Children, 1986.

Siks, Geraldine Brain. *Drama with Children*. New York: Harper, 1977.

Singer, Dorothy G., and Tracey A. Revenson. *A Piaget Primer: How a Child Thinks*. New York: New American Library, 1978.

Smith, Frank. *Reading without Nonsense*. New York: Columbia University Teachers College Press, 1979.

———, and George A. Miller. *The Genesis of Language*. Cambridge, Mass.: M.I.T. Press, 1966.

Stallibrass, Alison. *The Self-Respecting Child: Development through Spontaneous Play*. Foreword by John Holt. Reading, Mass.: Addison-Wesley, 1989.

Stone, L. Joseph, and Joseph Church. *Childhood and Adolescence: A Psychology of the Growing Person*. New York: Random House, 1964.

Strickland, Dorothy S., and Lesley Mandel Morrow, eds. *Emerging Literacy: Young Children Learn to Read and Write*. Newark, Del.: International Reading Assoc., 1989.

Sumner, Clarence W. *The Birthright of Babyhood*. New York: Thomas Nelson and Sons, 1936.

Taylor, Denny. *Family Literacy: Young Children Learning to Read and Write*. Portsmouth, N.H.: Heinemann, 1983.

_____, and Dorothy S. Strickland. *Family Storybook Reading.* Portsmouth, N.H.: Heinemann, 1986.

Teale, William H., and Elizabeth Sulzby, eds. *Emergent Literacy: Writing and Reading.* Norwood, N.J.: Ablex, 1986.

Thomas, James L. *Play, Learn, and Grow: An Annotated Guide to the Best Books and Materials for Very Young Children.* New York: R.R. Bowker, 1991.

Vygotsky, L. S. *Thought and Language.* New York: Wiley, 1962.

Wells, Gordon. *The Meaning Makers: Children Learning Language and Using Language to Learn.* Portsmouth, N.H.: Heinemann, 1986.

White, Burton L. *Educating the Infant and Toddler.* Lexington, Mass.: Lexington Books, 1988.

White, Dorothy. *Books before Five.* New York: Heinemann, 1986 (reprint).

Articles and Brochures

Association for Library Service to Children. *Programming for Very Young Children.* Program Support Publication, no. 1. Chicago: American Library Association, 1980.

Baer-Lindsay, Christopher. "Library Programming for Toddlers." *Public Libraries* 22:3 (Fall 1983): 111–13.

Butler, Dorothy. "Saying It Louder." *School Library Journal* 35:13 (September 1989): 155–59.

Cannon, Helen Wiley, and Joyce Dixon. "Parents, New Babies, and Books." *School Library Journal* 24:5 (January 1978): 68 (Practically Speaking column).

Clancy, Jeanne Marie. "Board Books Come of Age." *School Library Journal* 35:11 (July 1989): 34–35.

Cullinan, Bernice E., Ellin Greene, and Angela M. Jaggar. "Books, Babies, and Libraries: The Librarian's Role in Literacy Development." *Language Arts* 67:7 (November 1990): 750–55.

Elsmo, Nancy, and Micki Nevett. "The Public Library: A Resource Center for Parents: A Drama in Three Acts." *Public Libraries* 22:3 (Fall 1983): 96–98.

Farnsworth, Kathryn. "Parents as Partners." *New Jersey Libraries* 13 (December 1980–January 1981): 11–13.

Feinberg, Sandra. "The Parent/Child Workshop: A Unique Program." *School Library Journal* 31:8 (April 1985): 38–41.

_____. "The Parent/Child Workshop: A Unique Library Program for Parents and Babies." *Public Libraries* 24:4 (Winter 1985): 143–45.

Greene, Ellin. "Early Childhood Centers: Three Models." *School Library Journal* 30:6 (February 1984): 21–27.

_____, and Bernice E. Cullinan. "Educating Librarians to Serve Early Childhood." *School Library Journal* 34:11 (August 1988): 54 (Make Your Point column).

Heath, Shirley B. "What No Bedtime Story Means: Narrative Skills at Home and School." *Language and Society* 2 (April 1982): 49–76.

Jeffery, Debby, and Ellen Mahoney. "Sitting Pretty: Infants, Toddlers, and Lapsits." *School Library Journal* 35:8 (April 1989): 37–39.

Kewish, Nancy. "South Euclid's Pilot Project for Two-Year-Olds and Parents." *School Library Journal* 25:7 (March 1979): 93–98.

Lamme, Linda Leonard, and Athol B. Packer. "Bookreading Behaviors of Infants." *The Reading Teacher* 39:6 (February 1986): 504–09.

Locke, Jill L. "Pittsburgh's Beginning with Books Project." *School Library Journal* 34:6 (February 1988): 22–24.

Markowsky, Juliet Kellogg. "Storytime for Toddlers." *School Library Journal* 33:9 (May 1977): 28–31.

Ormerod, Jan. "Designing Books for Babies and Young Children." *The Children's Literature Council of Pennsylvania* 3:2 (1989): 3–6.

Ponish, Karen. " 'Babywise' and Toys Develop Literacy Skills." *American Libraries* 18:8 (September 1987): 709–10 (Youthreach column).

Sivulich, Kenneth G., and Sandra Sivulich. "Media Library for Preschoolers: A Service of the Erie Metropolitan Library." *Top of the News* 31:1 (November 1974): 49–54.

Smardo, Frances A. "Are Librarians Prepared to Serve Young Children?" *Journal of Education for Librarianship* 20:4 (Spring 1980): 274–84.

_____. "Public Library Programs for Young Children: A Review of the Research and Descriptive Literature." *Public Library Quarterly* 1:2 (Summer 1979): 187–207.

_____. "Public Library Services for Young Children in Day Care and Their Caregivers." *Public Library Quarterly* 7:1/2 (Spring/Summer 1986): 45–56.

Teale, William. "Parents Reading to Their Children: What We Know and Need to Know." *Language Arts* 58:8 (November/December 1981): 903–12.

_____. "Positive Environments for Learning to Read: What Studies of Early Readers Tell Us." *Language Arts* 55:8 (November/December 1978): 922–32.

Terwilliger, Gail. "A Sampling of Parent Education Programs." *Public Libraries* 23:2 (Summer 1984): 54–56.

Towey, Cathleen A. "Babywise: Booking a Head Start for Parents." *School Library Journal* 36:9 (September 1990): 148–52.

Toys: Tools for Learning. Washington, D.C.: National Association for the Education of Young Children, 1985.

Walsh, Joseph A. "Parenting Programs in Libraries." *School Library Journal* 29:6 (February 1983): 32–35.

Witkin, Lynne J. "Mothers' Discussion Groups in Public Libraries." *Social Work* 21:6 (November 1976): 525–26.

Witty, Margot, ed. "The Child's Mind." *Harpers Magazine* 256 (April 1978): 43–58.

Yucht, Alice. "Children's Services Helping Parents." *New Jersey Libraries* 13 (December 1980–January 1981): 13–15.

Professional Journals and Newsletters

ACEI Exchange
Association for Childhood
Education International
11141 Georgia Avenue
Suite 200
Wheaton, MD 20902

Caring
332 S. Michigan Avenue
Suite 1250
Chicago, IL 60604

CDF Reports
Children's Defense Fund
P.O. Box 7584
Washington, DC 20077-1245

*Center for Parent Education
Newsletter*
Center for Parent Education
55 Chapel Street
Newton, MA 02160

Child Development
Society for Research in Child
Development
University of Chicago Press
Journals Division
P.O. Box 37005
Chicago, IL 60637

Childhood Education
Journal of the Association for
Childhood Education
International
11141 George Avenue
Suite 200
Wheaton, MD 20902

Daycare & Early Education
Human Sciences Press, Inc.
233 Spring Street
New York, NY 10013-1578

Day Care U.S.A. Newsletter
8701 Georgia Avenue
Suite 800
Silver Spring, MD 20910

Early Years
P.O. Box 912
Farmingdale, NY 11735

Exceptional Children
Council for Exceptional Children
1920 Association Drive
Reston, VA 22091-1589

Gifted Child Quarterly
National Association for Gifted
Children
5100 N. Edgewood Drive
St. Paul, MN 55112

High Scope Resource
The High/Scope Press
Educational Research Foundation
600 N. River Street
Upsilanti, MI 48198

Young Children
National Association for the
Education of Young Children
1834 Connecticut Avenue, NW
Washington, DC 20009

EARLY CHILDHOOD
CONFERENCE MATERIALS

Books, Babies, and Libraries:
Making the Connection

April 13–15, 1989

Conference Program

Thursday, April 13

6:30–8:30 p.m.   **Opening Reception**
Celeste Bartos Forum, NYPL
Presiding: Julie Cummins
Greetings: Harold W. McGraw, Jr.
                 Dr. John Brademas
Introduction: Dr. Ellin Greene
Speaker: Dorothy Butler

Friday, April 14

8:30–9:10 a.m.   **Registration and Coffee**
Main Building, New York University

9:15–10:30 a.m.   **Opening Session**
Auditorium, Main Building, NYU
Presiding: Dr. Ellin Greene
Welcome: Dr. Robert A. Burnham
Introduction: Dr. Bernice E. Cullinan
Speaker: Dr. Lawrence Balter

10:30–10:45 a.m.   **Mini-break**

10:45–12 noon   **Small Group Discussions**

159

12:15–1:30 p.m.	**Buffet Luncheon** Eisner and Lubin Auditorium Loeb Student Center, NYU
1:30–1:45 p.m.	**Spotlight on the New York Public Library Early Childhood Resource and Information Center** Presenter: Hannah Nuba
1:45–3:00 p.m.	**Panel Discussion: Networking/Education for Library Service to Early Childhood** Presiding: Barbara Rollock Panelists: Dr. Ann Carlson, Dr. Carol Millsom, Dr. William Teale, Dr. Burton L. White
3:00–3:25 p.m.	**Leisurely Walk to ECRIC**
3:30–4:30 p.m.	**Ella Jenkins Workshop** ECRIC Auditorium Presiding: Hannah Nuba
4:30–4:45 p.m.	**Evaluation and Closing Remarks** Presiding: Julie Cummins
4:45–5:45 p.m.	**Closing Reception** Early Childhood Resource and Information Center, NYPL
Saturday, April 15	**Post-Conference Activities**
10:00 a.m.–12 noon	**Panel Discussion: The Image and the Word: the Role of Nursery Rhymes, Picture Books, and Film in Early Language Development** Bankers Trust Company Auditorium, Donnell Library Center, NYPL Presiding: Despina Croussouloudis Panelists: Dorothy Butler, Maureen Gaffney, Dr. Angela Jaggar, Jan Ormerod
10:30–11:30 a.m.	**Ella Jenkins in Concert** Early Childhood Resource and Information Center, NYPL Presiding: Hannah Nuba

Saying It Louder

by Dorothy Butler

Several months ago I started to think about what I might say to you today, and found myself in something of a quandary. Your brief was generously wide, inviting me to "feel free to be anecdotal"—a clear sign that the writer of the letter had read my books and knew about my tendency to gossip. Of course, the letter also drew my attention to the fact that the concern of this conference was to find more and better ways of "making the connection between books, babies, and libraries."

"What can I possibly say that hasn't been said already?" I asked my daughter, Chris, who I was visiting at the time. "Nothing, probably," she answered with brutal economy. "You just have to say it *louder.*" She was, of course, quite right. We are not short of *theory* in this field; it is the tools with which the theory might be implemented that we seem to lack. I spared Chris my depressing suspicion that the outlook is less than rosy—that those of us who have been saying for years that children must make early contact with books if the glue is to stick are hardly even holding our own, let alone making headway. She needs all the strength and good cheer she can conjure up in her busy life as teacher, counselor, wife and mother of three school-age children, not gloomy prognostications from her own mother.

Let me pause for a moment, though, in case you feel that this address could turn into a lugubrious lament. Let me offer my first anecdote, gleaned in this same daughter's home a few minutes after the above conversation.

Some of you may recall my reference to a two-year-old called Anthony in the early chapters of *Babies Need Books*. This once chubby little chap, now a skinny, near-thirteen-year-old, is in his first year at high school. He is the eldest of Chris's three children, and, because he is one of my favorite people, I care very much that his new school, which he entered only a few weeks ago, should prove to serve his needs as well as his first school did. So I asked him how things were going.

Quite unself-consciously, he showed me an exercise book in which he is obliged to record his impressions of life in general, and school in particular, as part of his English language course. I read his first entries with interest. With the fluency I might have expected from this particular child, Anthony had touched on his personal concerns about making friends and getting used to new routines. What took my attention and touched my heart immediately, however, was his early complaint that the school library was not, in the first week, open at lunchtime; in the second, his satisfaction that it *was*; in the third week his exasperation that it was never, apparently, to be open during mid-morning break; and in his latest entry, the hope that it might be possible to organize a petition for the reversal of this outrageous injustice!

Now, this is a boy who loves camping and tramping, makes energetic use of his bike and skateboard, builds and repairs things with skill, swims and plays cricket and soccer with style. That *books* owned and borrowed are

SLJ 35:13 (September 1989): 155–59. Reprinted by permission of *School Library Journal.*

part of Anthony's very being is his own good fortune. One can see how they both support and extend his experience of people, and the world. Surely, this is what we want for all children.

Before I settle down to consider the ways and means by which libraries—and schools too, I believe—must address themselves to the recruitment of the babies and toddlers in their neighborhoods to books, I should like to look a little more closely at the benefits of a book-based life.

On all fronts we hear of the advantages to children of electronic equipment, the purchase of which, by schools and libraries, inevitably reduces the funds available for buying books. The unique capacity of the book for transmitting nourishment to the mind and spirit is increasingly unrecognized.

Facts are seen as all-important—and the easiest way to produce a fact is to press a button. I am moved to join T. S. Eliot in his plea: "Where is the wisdom we have lost in knowledge? Where is the knowledge we have lost in information?"

There is strong justification for the fear that most of the population is not aware of any loss. How can one experience loss if one has not experienced possession? And herein lies our greatest problem. How to tell such people that electronic contraptions cannot perform miracles, that the state of children's minds and imaginations is more important than the equipment in their schools or homes—and that language is the magic component? Language—the raw material of thought, the tool used by that incomparable computer, the human brain, to reflect, deduce and innovate—has been, in my lifetime, swept aside, subordinated, as an instrument of education, to inert machinery which, we are supposed to believe, will solve all our problems. Resourceful, expansive, living language, adequate for the purposes of Shakespeare and Galileo, Dickens and Einstein, is judged inadequate for the purposes of the modern world.

The ironical truth is, of course, that the highly literate child is likely to be the one who performs best on the computer keyboard anyway, not to mention his other greater exercise of discrimination in television and video-viewing. The child whose access to books is assured and accepted sees things in perspective, and is unlikely to be seduced into dull dependence on a flickering TV screen. This child is likely to recognize the shoddy—to employ a developing faculty of judgement, to want to tap the diverse resources of the *real world*. That there is an inherent unfairness in this must be admitted. Deprived of the literature of their culture—their birthright, that unique source of information and pleasure—many millions of the world's children are exposed to the crippling effects of the all-too-readily-available television screen. For these children, ours is a crime of both omission and commission.

At the State University of New York in 1984, Robert McNeil said of this influence: "I think this society is being force-fed with trivial fare, and I fear that the effects on our habits of mind, our language, our tolerance for effort and our appetite for complexity, are only dimly perceived." I could not help but smile nostalgically at McNeil's use of that old phrase *habit of mind*. Does anyone know what it means any longer? My parents' generation used it to describe the flavor or bent of an individual's habitual thought processes. Not only has the expression disappeared, nothing has taken its place. *I.Q.* is quite different.

Kathleen Jamieson, communications professor at the University of Texas, might have been speaking of my country, as well as of yours, when she said recently that "the nation's cultural education now is commercial advertisements and primetime sitcoms and dramas; there isn't the kind of depth and richness that a study of history, the Bible, Shakespeare brought into cultural literacy in the past. And so, the grounds on which we are building argument [and here she was referring to the making of political and social decisions], is in some way substantially impoverished."

The truth is that many millions of children will be condemned to the new so-called "visual literacy" (which does not include books as we have known them in the past); their sentence has been determined by those features of the world we have created which will coarsen their tastes with banal images and strident sound in the earliest and most impressionable days.

Babies and small children need precision, beauty, lilt and rhythm, and the opportunity to look and to listen, both at will and at length, as well as to touch and feel and smell. Words are finely tuned instruments which must be encountered early if their shades of meaning are to serve the developing intellect and emotions. There must be a two-way flow. There is no substitute for the loving exchange between adult and baby, each determined to communicate by whatever method springs to mind and hand. Lifelong habits are entrenched in this apparently simple exchange.

In *Babies Need Books,* I said that "books can be bridges between children and parents, and children and the world." That simple statement, made nearly ten years ago, has been said and resaid countless times in the years between. I was certainly not the first to say it, in one way or another; my early parenthood, beginning over forty years ago, was enriched and informed by the work of my countrywoman, Dorothy Neal White, and by notable Americans such as Paul Hazard, May Hill Arbuthnot and Ruth Hill Viguers, with the English writers and critics Margery Fisher, Roger Lancelyn Greene and others on hand when I needed them for reference. What they all gave me, more importantly, was the priceless gift of stimulation, reaffirming my own conviction that children's very beings would be nurtured and sustained through story, and that the adults in their lives had a central role to play in the process.

In those halcyon days, through the fifties and sixties (which saw such a burgeoning of children's literature on both sides of the Atlantic), I imagined that we needed only time, hard work and faith. Within another decade or two, the children of the world, deluged as they were with books of irresistible attraction and quality, would all be *reading*—voluntarily, joyfully, responsively. That this sort of reading pre-supposed fluency did not strike me as a problem. I believed that motivation—determination to be numbered among the "real" readers—was the vital accelerant into the perfection of necessary skills. (I still believe this.) And these were heady days!

We seemed to have solved the problem of book provision. Paperbacks appeared in the thousands; picture books in all their magnificence were suddenly within reach of ordinary families. The more idealistic of us envisaged a time soon to come, when every ten-year-old would have a paperback novel protruding from the hip pocket of his or her jeans.

Somehow, it didn't happen. Surprisingly, the provision of books was not the cure-all my generation expected it to be. I am haunted by a vision of a million bored children, their backs turned to a mountain of books—glorious books which would set their eyes sparkling, their hands grabbing, if only they could be encouraged to wade in.

We must face the fact that we have somehow failed to forge a link between these children and reading. For whatever reason, the connection is not there. What has gone wrong?

If we (and, of course, teachers) consider school-age children, we must admit that our efforts will be successful only part of the time. Producing children who perform to their own age level on a reading test is not the same thing at all as producing "real" readers. The real reader knows no barrier between page and mind; the book ceases to be a thing of wood pulp and printer's ink and assumes a nature of its own. To quote Aidan Chambers:

> ...Literature in print transcends time and place and person. A book is a time-space machine; a three-dimensional object that has shape, weight, texture and smell, and even taste. And compressed into those abstract marks made on paper, it carries, by a mystery we still do not understand, a cargo of the deepest knowledge of one person delivered directly to the most secret life of another, who may be many hundreds of miles away and many years of time distant.

A thought occurs which is laughably obvious if we come to consider it, but is commonly overlooked: the book as we know it has not changed in form or function since its invention. The first person all those centuries ago who abandoned the awkward rolled scroll, apportioned work to pages, and finally bound them on one side so that they could be read in smooth succession, must have been a genius. Only the invention of the wheel compares. And like the wheel, which has never changed in shape, the book has never altered in basic form. As a vehicle for that mysterious "cargo of the deepest knowledge of one person" (to use Chambers's expression), it performs impeccably.

Why, then, do we find it so hard, in our modern setting, to ensure that books are received by children—seen by them—as conveyors of wonder, delight and excitement? This is not the place to examine this question in depth. Suffice to say that modern children, seduced from birth by a society which dazes while it entertains, ignores the omnipotence of language as a force of life, and scorns old-fashioned notions like the deferment of gratification and the gathering of wisdom—these children are receiving shabby treatment from those they trust. We are to blame. We find it hard—impossible in some cases—to weld child and book together because we don't do it soon enough. We allow other pernicious influences to gain sway in children's preferences and then, panicking, cast around for someone or some institution to blame.

Our commonest object of censure in this connection is the school. Yet we know from our own experience, from the findings of research and the conclusions of commissions, that children who come to school with active minds, well-developed capacities for self-expression, and burgeoning vocabularies seem to slide into reading effortlessly, naturally.

The process should be natural. In learning to read, being "at home" with books, knowing how they work to convey information and to tell stories, is the fundamental first step. Learning to read, in Marie Clay's phrase, is "getting the message." Children will extract "the message" from written prose with the same determination they use to glean meaning from spoken language—if the game can be shown to be worth the candle. And it can be— as it is for the lucky children who fall into the category described above, those for whom books are playfellows and bedfellows from babyhood. We must find ways to reach the babies and toddlers of our world if we hope seriously to increase the ranks of the real readers.

Our only direct route to children that don't read is probably through parents—and for "parents" one can usually read "mothers." Of course there is reason for satisfaction—for joy—if daycare centers and nursery schools include books in their programs. But, like schools, they are institutions that children go to. Real and lasting impressions come from the home. Certainly there are those children who will seize the first book they ever encounter in nursery or primary school, hurl themselves into the reading game, and astonish everyone by embarking on book-centered lives.

They are the exceptions. For every such child—and the phenomenon occurs in the art and music fields, too—there are thousands of children who could have been recruited, and were not. These children are exposed to books at school, may be involved in lively reading programs run by dedicated teachers, but they still bypass books and settle for the uncertain, often mindless gratification of the television screen.

Evidence abounds that lasting changes must be generated in children's homes if they are to occur at all. Short-term effects certainly flow from school programs energetically pursued at every level—and we can be surprised, on occasion.

Let us never become so disillusioned that we abandon any avenue. But until we can reach into homes, and actually change the nature of their influence on children's developing tastes, it is unlikely that we will markedly change the proportion of readers in our community. In fact, in the face of the growing influence of factors already mentioned which combine to convince children that reading is a dull and difficult pastime—certainly not an attractive occupation for out-of-school leisure time—it is likely that the situation will worsen.

I believe that public libraries constitute a unique bastion in this dismal scene. Their one overriding advantage is that they actually exist for the purpose of meeting the assumed reading needs of every member of the community they serve, regardless of age, sex, race, social class or intellectual level. This is not to say that libraries have in the past accomplished this, or that they are all doing so now. But the capacity to serve, however under-realized, still constitutes a powerful potential tool for the reversal of trends in people's lives.

But, still, *potential*. Why not *actual*? What would we need to do to empower libraries to play their real, intended role in people's lives? Particularly in children's lives?

Let's look at public libraries—and of course, my conversance is with those in my own country. We have made enormous strides in the physical attributes of the libraries themselves. The high-ceilinged, cold, awesome buildings of my childhood have been replaced with warm, light, welcoming complexes in which the children's department, even if small, has cushions on the mats, books in low bins for easy access, and puzzles, puppets and stuffed toys to make small borrowers feel at home. The children who do come—remembering that babies and toddlers must be brought by parents—exploit these benefits to the fullest. Little can be said in criticism of the system from the point of view of these privileged children.

Librarians then? In my day they tended to be austere, unsmiling people dedicated to preserving books, rather than to serving people—and children must have posed problems in rooms ostensibly devoted to scholarship, rooms in which notices on the wall said, starkly, SILENCE.

My own children had much better luck, encountering that priceless blessing, a kind and friendly librarian who remained in place from the days of their babyhood until their passage into adulthood. Indeed, the garden around the Birkenhead Library was later named the "Nell Fisher Reserve"; I never drive past without remembering her. My grown children acknowledge her as a strong influence on their lives.

Miss Fisher had her own way of reserving a special book for a special child; she would rummage under her desk, and then slip it almost furtively into a child's hands: a secret treat, no less. Once, one of my children came in from school with the news that he had to walk back to the shopping center to buy some India ink for the map he was drawing. He had passed the shop, but had had no money with him. He was ten years old and the winter evening was already drawing in—but off he went. An hour later when I was starting to feel a little worried, he came in and his face was shining. "Miss Fisher had *Pigeon Post* for me!" he said jubilantly. "Good," said I. "Did you get your ink?" His expression changed to one of ludicrous dismay. "Heck! I forgot!" The lure of the library had been his undoing—but the influence of Arthur Ransome on his life more than compensated, we both believed, though we did not discuss the matter. (A friend down the road lent him some India ink and I ultimately took *Pigeon Post* into custody against an all-night stand, which might not have included map drawing.)

We all have our favorite tales to tell; but we are the favored ones—"on the side of the angels," as Forster would describe us. For each of us there are many thousands who do not see their local library as an extension of their living rooms, who do not pass on the comfortable habit of library visiting to their children. And it is from parents that children will learn, whatever the lesson.

We can safely say, then, that in your country and mine we have excellent children's libraries, suitably furnished and well-stocked (though no library ever has enough books, and provision is seldom high on the list of governmental priority). In the main, we have well-trained librarians who understand children's needs and are increasingly accepting of children as they are: noisy, sometimes insubordinate, setting no great store by order or timetable, but also honest, friendly, and full of such willing good cheer that the heart sometimes aches for them, given the state of the world we sentence them to live in.

The problem, then, does not lie predominantly with personnel or institutions. It is one of connection. There seems to be an invisible wall between a huge section of the populace and the libraries which hope to serve it. The seduction of apparently easier, all-too-available entertainment is not merely a deterrent to library enrollment, either. It is a cause of a crippling complaint which will keep its sufferers from books for life: the inability to read fluently enough to make the exercise worthwhile.

One is not *reading* in any rewarding sense until meaning pours, without apparent effort on the reader's part, from page to mind. I like J.B. Kerfoot's analogy of responsive readers taking the text for their scenario and producing it on the stage of their own imaginations, with resources furnished by their own experience of life. This sort of reading is like listening, another skill which—alas!—is being eroded by the day in our society. Further, the reader must "reach out," as Martin Buber's phrase, to meet the author, if maximum satisfaction and understanding is to be achieved.

The active use of mind and imagination required for this sort of reading demands an investment of self, an assumption that the rewards will be positive. How hard this is to implant if those other lures are given full rein in the early years, without competition from the experience of story between covers! How easy, if print and picture have been shared, with delight, from birth!

Last year, when she was two, my granddaughter Bridget asked me for "Humpty Dumpty" from her *Mother Goose* book. "You find it," I said, busy with something else. Quite soon, "Here's Humpy Dumpy," said Bridget, having found the right page. But she was pointing to the text, not the picture! "You read it," I said then—and she did, her finger moving indiscriminately over the words, without a glance at the picture. By heart, of course, but with total, untaught understanding of the way written language works to produce meaning.

And so we go round in circles. Children must expect to become readers— *want* to become readers. Observe the example of adults who read with enjoyment, and who have time and space in their lives to read, before they are likely to embark on the long hours of "practice" which will ensure the sort of fluency which this state demands. We know what the requirements are; we know that children exposed to written language from birth are unconsciously noting the patterns, the conventions of the text. They have a head start, but it is an advantage which only a close adult can confer.

Even once school days begin, children spend more than three times as long awake, in their parents' care, as they spend at school. It is parents who are powerful. They must be reached, convinced, and helped to exercise this power. And, in this connection, enlightened public libraries which have no "age of entry" have a clear advantage over schools to reach and influence. Achieving this access must be the concern of every public library which hopes to continue to exist. Bluntly, if the readers dry up, the libraries close down!

No prescription will suit all situations; methods and programs will be as various as the people and institutions involved. High on the list must be the raising of public awareness that "reading matters," that books are unlikely to become part of a person's entrenched way of life unless encountered early, and that school entry as a time to meet books is too late by five or six years.

Most importantly, those authorities who are seen by the public (however mistakenly) as oracular, must be persuaded to utter convincing exhortations on the subject of books and reading to the community at large. Campaigns run by local governments, backed by business interests, supported in principle by schools and in practical ways by libraries, to reach the parents of newborn babies in maternity hospitals—with vigorous follow-up—might be expected to bear fruit. And indeed, have done so already. I know of several energetic programs; the Orlando Public Library's "Catch 'em in the Cradle" venture first alerted me to their possibilities.

We still need, in all societies, the conversion of governmental authorities to the view that the funding of such schemes is a matter of national importance. We know that children are the citizens of tomorrow; that the horrifying problems we have created on social and environmental fronts will be theirs, not ours, to cope with. Why then, do we still treat children as second-class citizens, whatever lip service we give to our concern for them? As a society, we undervalue children; worse, we work very hard to divest them of their inexhaustible energy, their fresh creativity, their astonishing faith in us.

Empowerment of parents must be central to any scheme for change in children's lives, and this must mean more than access to financial help. Somehow, parents must be persuaded, not only of their responsibility to their children from birth, but of their own incomparable power in their children's lives. Parents must be brought to believe further that this power to influence has nothing to do with the wish to influence. They will influence their children, whether they intend to or not. They must be convinced that their love for their children will be their children's greatest strength, that unconditional human love is the most priceless of all human gifts, and that the capacity to give it has nothing to do with wealth, position, or education. They must come to know that their children will learn from them the capacity to love and relate to other people and that no other lesson will ever be as important as this one.

Frustratingly, one of the greatest stumbling blocks to success in this project is *simplicity*. Great changes are thought to require complex technology and huge sums of money. The simple triangle of parent, child, and book is not easily accepted as the passport it actually is to the essential qualities of life: the human capacities to love, laugh, and to learn. This is not likely to begin to change until support for a "Books from Birth" campaign is given, with appropriate fanfare by the "powers that be." This, while only a start, would be an important one.

Our lobby, therefore, must be to these "powers" as well as to parents. Ways must be found—and will be found—if our resolution is strong enough, our case conclusive enough, our voices heard often enough.

Children are our greatest resource. They must be helped to grow strong in spirit if our world—their world—is to become a better place. Their own survival may well depend on it. You and I know that this strength can flow from books, that language is the key to our humanity, that narrative language is the vehicle by which we order our thoughts, and that these are the things we must give our children. Our cause is not peripheral to the urgent causes of the world; it is central.

C.S. Lewis said that "through literature we become a thousand people and yet remain ourselves"; and I think my grandson, an ordinary kid in baggy beach shorts and yellow tee-shirt in Auckland, New Zealand, is simultaneously Jason among the Argonauts in search of the Golden Fleece; Chas McGill in wartime England, desperately concealing a Nazi gunner from parents and authorities, imperceptibly growing up amid the anguish, thrill and futility of it all; Beric, Rosemary Sutcliff's "outcast" in Roman Britain, knowing rejection, starting to understand prejudice—but courage, and love, too—and Sam, on his side of the mountain, determined to make his own, solitary way. Then three-year-old Bridget, his cousin, astride the verandah rail, chanting "Rumpeta, rumpeta, rumpeta," clearly inside the skin of one of that assorted band which accompanied the Bad Baby on his rollicking adventure on the elephant's back...

A boy and a girl, ten years apart in age, looking at the world through other people's eyes, yet seeing clearly with their own.

Once again Aidan Chambers says for me what I want to say: "While we can tell each other what is going on inside us and be told what is going on inside other people, we remain human, sane, hopeful, creative. In short, we remain alive."

Designing Books for Babies and Young Children

by Jan Ormerod

Most of my books for babies and young children are the result of close observation and recording of the day-to-day activities of children. For example, my first Baby Book Series was born out of watching my small daughter, Laura, and her young cat exploring their environment. The cat seemed to be at about the same developmental stage as she. They would approach a saucepan in the same way—sniff it, taste it, tap it, hop inside it, sit on it— explore it in the same sensory fashion.

Book ideas began to grow, and then, in a dummy book about the cat and baby opening a present (preferring the wrapping paper, ribbon, and box to the present itself), a dad appeared. The present idea never came to fruition, but the stories about the father, baby, and cat became my first Baby Books Series, *Dad's Back, Messy Baby, Reading,* and *Sleeping.*

In *Messy Baby,* the toddler follows Dad about, undoing all the tidying up. Daddy says "clothes in the cupboard" while the baby busily takes all the books the father has just put on the shelf onto the floor. Every picture book page offers many alternatives. Each one is thought about, drawn about, and a decision is made. My task as a storyteller using pictures is to observe, record, and edit. Images need to be sifted and organized. Telling a story in pictures is a little like watching a movie, then selecting out the evocative moment, like a still image from a film. I need to capture the moment which has clarity and simplicity, invites empathy, and allows the reader to bring her own knowledge to that moment to enrich it and develop it according to her life experiences.

Reprinted from *Journal of the Children's Literature Council* 3:2 (1989) 3–6; based on a slide presentation given April 15, 1989, as part of the NYPL/NYU Early Childhood Conference. Reprinted by permission of the Children's Literature Council of Pennsylvania. The illustrations from *Messy Baby* (above) and *The Saucepan Game* by Jan Ormerod are reprinted by permission of Lothrop, Lee and Shepard Books, a division of William Morrow & Company, Inc.

Several years on, the original concept of cat, baby, and saucepan has been revived in a book called *The Saucepan Game.* It is a personal favorite of mine. I was aiming for:

a. **economy:** a very simple story
b. **clarity:** drawings that were clear and informative
c. **humor:** which invites empathy
d. a quality I can only label **space:** space for the child and adult to enrich the story by bringing their understandings to the book and sharing their experiences

A more recent book, *Kitten Day,* is the result of watching little Laura, five years later, longingly waiting for the arrival of a new kitten. She had chosen

it some weeks before but needed to wait till it was ready to leave its litter to become her kitten. She drew a heart on the calendar around the date of its arrival and wrote "kitten day" in crayon. As I watched the kitten's arrival and watched their relationship develop, I realized I was observing something universal and important—the tender empathy of a young child for another small vulnerable creature, and the comfort of such companionship.

There are few situations a child is likely to face that are not dealt with in books. Books open windows, giving glimpses of other worlds, other situations, other people. Some may evoke recognition, others show the actions of people who behave differently from anything the child has experienced. Some of the "lessons" books offer are quite specific, but others are a great deal more subtle. They sidle in without the child's being entirely aware of what she's learning. These are the lessons which may never be talked about, but the memories of which may linger and affect behavior for a lifetime.

I design books for children and adults in equal part because I depend on an adult to create the right atmosphere to share the book. I believe a parent, teacher, or librarian can have fun identifying with the adult in the book, while the child sees the book at *her* level. Such books have a double benefit—the adult who shares them with the child will feel such enjoyment that it will spill over into the whole occasion, and while still remaining children's books, they allow the child to step outside her own experiences and understand the adult's point of view.

The most important thing, I believe, about books for babies and very young children is that they are shared between the child and a caring adult. It is a time for physical closeness and comfort, of quiet and harmony, of sharing ideas and emotions, laughing and learning together. The learning and benefit that take place are not only enjoyed by the child. Any adult who takes time to share books with small children will be rewarded, enriched, and revitalized by it, every time.

I cannot speak about language acquisition in the very young with any authority. All I can share with you is my instinct, my intuition, my gut feeling that sharing books, rhymes, and pictures is one of the richest experiences we can offer young children, and one of the most rewarding experiences we can offer ourselves.

SUBJECT INDEX

Prepared by Janet Russell

AUTHOR-TITLE INDEX

Prepared by Interface Group

A former associate professor at the University of Chicago Graduate Library School, Ellin Greene is a nationally known consultant in library services for children, storyteller, author, workshop leader, and conference director. She was consultant/director for the New York Public Library Early Childhood Project, funded by a grant from the Carnegie Corporation of New York, 1987–89. Greene is a frequent contributor to professional journals and co-author (with Augusta Baker) of *Storytelling: Art and Technique* (Bowker, 1987).